Key to Symbols Used in Text Margin and on Maps

⚑	Golf facilities		Church/Ecclesiastical site
∏	Archaeological site		Building of interest
✻	Garden		Castle/Fortification
♣	Parkland		Museum/Art gallery
▯	Industrial Archaeology		Beautiful view/Scenery, Natural phenomenon
🦆	Birdlife		Other place of interest
🚶	Recommended walk		

Key to Maps

——	Main road	⬭	Lake
═══	Motorway	- - - - -	County Boundary
⟋	River	⊓⊓⊓⊔	Hadrian's Wall (visible remains)
▬	Town/City	⊓ ⊓⊓⊔	Hadrian's Wall (non-visible remains)
●	Town		

Note on the Map

The maps draw[n] ... ...nsive, are not
designed to be u... ...cate the main
towns, villages and place of interest. ... ...overed by the
Ordnance Survey 1:50,000 (approximately 1in to $1^1/_4$ miles)
Landranger Series; sheets 74, 75, 80, 81, 86, 87, 88, 92, 93 and 94. For
more general purposes the Ordnance Survey Touring Map and
Guide, Sheet 14 (1in to $2^1/_2$ miles) is recommended.

INDEX TO 1:50 000 MAPS OF GREAT BRITAIN

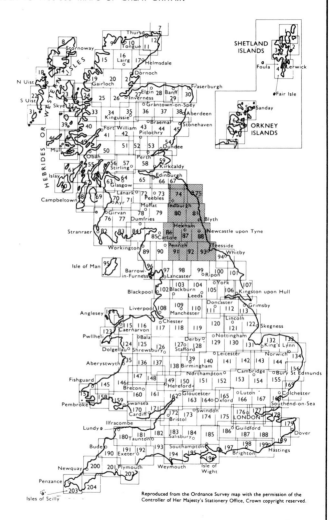

**Shading indicates Ordnance Survey maps recommended
for use in conjunction with this guide**

CONTENTS

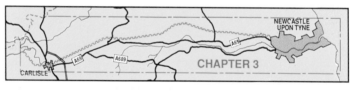

INTRODUCTION

N orthumbria has been called the 'best kept secret in England'. While that statement might be a little extravagant, it is true to say that for a long time the region was only known to a comparative handful of outsiders. Even now it is possible to tour on quiet side roads free from the traffic problems which beset the more popular parts of Britain. The freedom of its sandy beaches can be yours alone, and queueing to visit one of the stately homes or border castles is virtually unknown. Museums and visitor centres encapsulate Northumbria's history, from the bloody days of border warfare to the changing face of industry. Contrary to preconceived opinion, the weather is surprisingly good, admittedly sharper than say Devon and Cornwall, but all the better for that.

At one time Northumbria was a kingdom stretching from Strathclyde to the Humber. Much of Britain's early history took place within those bounds, and England's Christianity developed from a fragile hold along the north-east coast. Today, Northumbria covers the counties of Northumberland, Tyne and Wear, County Durham and Cleveland. This guide is therefore devoted to the modern geographical bounds of Northumbria.

What is Northumbria?

The region divides itself comfortably within the confines of its political boundaries. **Northumberland** is mostly an agricultural county, with sheep farming or forestry around the wild moors, and arable farming occupying the more fertile lands further east. Small-scale fishing still occupies many of the inhabitants along the coast; their activities are mostly inshore, fishing for crabs and lobsters and sea salmon as the season dictates. Prosperous market towns act as focal points for people whose livelihoods depend on farming. Many of the castles built to protect those livelihoods were made into homes more in keeping with modern needs by Victorian architects, and one, Alnwick, is still lived in by the descendants of Shakespeare's 'Harry Hotspur', Lord Percy. Most of the north-western side of the county is now part of the Northumberland National Park which is administered from Hexham. The character of the park ranges from the wild moorlands of the Cheviot Hills to the fascinating links with the Roman occupation around Hadrian's Wall. Adjacent to the park is Kielder Forest, the largest man-made forest in Europe, and also Kielder Water, the largest man-made lake.

Heavy industry is mostly confined to **Tyne and Wear**, vastly changed yet based on foundations laid by industrial geniuses like Armstrong and Parsons. Coal is no longer produced on a scale which created the wealth behind many of the stately homes. Steel furnaces no longer belch their flames into the night sky and like the coal industry, many of their sites have been put to other uses such as light industrial estates or shopping zones. Here was the home of two of the founding fathers of the railway system, George Stephenson and William Hedley.

Railways were developed to move both coal and iron-ore; their track-beds still snake across the Tyneside landscape, some carrying railways such as the Metro, others, if unwanted, converted into historical trails linked to industrial museums. Newcastle upon Tyne is the commercial heart of Tyne and Wear; ship building still occupies much of the lower Tyne, but gone are the days when massive liners built by the shipyards of Hebburn, Jarrow and Wallsend first ventured into the North Sea at the start of their maiden voyages. Today's vessels are more likely to be the fantastic structures which are towed out into the North Sea in the search for oil. Deep sea fishermen still use North Shields at the mouth of the river, but the descendants of the colourful fisherwives who processed their catch, are more than likely employed in one of the hi-tech factories of new towns like Cramlington which have sprung up along the coastal plain. It is always reckoned that the true 'Geordie' lives on Tyneside, but while there is no recognised boundary, if you want to hear the melodious lilt and dialect words which are probably more easily understood by Norwegians than people from Southern England, then go into the pubs and working men's clubs around the Tyne.

County Durham is a land of contrasts. Its dales flow from high wild Pennine moors only recently given the accolade of being an Area of Outstanding Natural Beauty. Such is their interest, untouched in recent decades, that the title gives them almost the same status as a National Park. The land around these dales has more or less recovered from the attentions of miners of both lead and iron ore, who took the riches beneath the ground with little thought of the future. Pitiful relics abound of many lifetimes' work and some, such as the Killhope Wheel Mining Centre have been preserved to explain the meaning of their labours. Monks who had carried the miraculously preserved body of St Cuthbert around the North of England for over a century, settled on a naturally defended crag above a tight meander of the River Wear and founded an abbey which eventually became the glorious cathedral of Durham. Constantly in the front line of wars between England and Scotland, Durham became the headquarters of a county palatinate or semi-autonomous region headed by Prince Bishops who ruled until 1836. Even now Bishops of Durham often act with an independance which is not always appreciated by those in higher authority.

Huge fortunes were created from the coal which lies beneath County Durham, but mining activity, like that beneath Tyneside, is now on a much reduced scale. Only a handful of super-efficient collieries remain in operation, and scattered throughout the county are small red-brick towns and villages desperately holding on to their identity after the closure of their life-sustaining coal mines. Nothing remains of a mile-long steel works which lit the night sky and stained the cottages of Consett with its grime. Landscaped slag heaps and light industry now cover the dead industry of a town which had its major artery severed. But all is not gloom and doom. New industries are flocking in to use the inbred skills of the Durham workforce; international companies and government offices have moved into prime sites around new towns like Washington and Peterlee. The industrial heritage is preserved in a number of interesting museums, but none compares with the Beamish Open Air Museum, a unique collection of buildings and restored machinery set in the open parkland of Beamish Hall, off the A693 near Stanley. Do not visit County Durham if you are looking for attractive beaches, for much of the coastline is spoilt by nearby collieries. With one or two notable exceptions, such as Trimdon or Castle Eden Denes, if you want bathing beaches you will have to look further north along the Northumbria coast, or south on either side of the Tees estuary.

Cleveland, the smallest area to be covered by this guide, is basically Teesside with an incursion onto the north-facing escarpment of the North York Moors. Teesside industry is two-fold: steel and chemicals, but both are based on an original alchemy which is rooted on the North York Moors. Iron ore was mined on the heights above Rosedale and carried down the steep escarpment by a complex system of railways and an incline to Middlesbrough, where it was converted into steel. The original furnaces have gone, but today's steel industry, the most modern and efficient in Europe, uses imported ore and is sited at Dorman's Town, conveniently near the deep water of the river's mouth. The chemical industry also has its links with the moors where for centuries alum was mined, as well as salt which lies deep beneath the northern banks of the Tees. Now highly specialised and certainly no longer using alum, Teesside's chemical and petroleum industry offers a weird sci-fi vision of fractionating columns and cooling towers, creating a strange but not un-attractive night sky.

The first fare-paying passenger-carrying railway ran between Stockton and Darlington. Middlesbrough developed on a grid system, the first 'new town' in England, but Cleveland is not all industry. The elegant Georgian centres of Darlington and Guisborough speak of a prosperity founded on agriculture rather than the heavy industry which came with the Industrial Revolution. As well as these hidden architectural gems, Cleveland has miles of clean sandy beaches on either side of the mouth of the Tees and only misses its claim to one of the quaintest fishing villages on the coast, Staithes, by the width of a narrow stream. The moors, edged by curious hills like Roseberry Topping, are close at hand, and upstream along the Tees lush agricultural land gradually gives way to the rugged upper reaches of Upper Teesdale.

GEOLOGY

Rocks which make the foundations of Northumbria have travelled far across the face of the earth. At one time they were part of a tropical paradise somewhere south of the equator, but movements of the earth's crust over millions of years shifted them into their present positions. Some of the oldest surface rocks are in the Cheviots, the eroded remains of rocks created by volcanic activity. Mingling with them are outcrops of granite which pushed their way through the ash of ancient volcanoes. Old as these rocks are, they sit on top of Silurian slates, themselves the deposited relics of even older rocks laid down in an ancient sea, part of the ever constant process of building up and wearing down. Gradually this volcanic land sank and a tropical sea surrounded what was to become the Cheviots. As the land continued to sink, the remains of countless millions of sea creatures and the plant life of this sea built up layers of limestones many hundreds of feet thick. These limestones formed two distinct types, Carboniferous which is to the west and Magnesian north of Teesside. The former stone is quarried in Weardale and made into cement or used as roadstone. Magnesian Limestone forms the interesting sea cliffs near Marsden Bay below South Shields, but further north it is also exploited for the chemical industry and specialist cements. Gradually a river delta began to fill this tropical sea with the muds and gravel from a long dead mountain range. These are now the shales and gritstones which generally form the Pennines and land to the east. About 220 million years ago a desert covered what was to become Teesside and it was during this period that salt and potash lakes were created. Alum, a complex salt of the phosphates of potasium and aluminium, occurs on the North York Moors, and was used as a mordant to 'fix' Turkey Red dyes; iron-ore deposits along the northern escarpment founded Middlesbrough's iron and steel industry. Neither of these deposits are used today, but salt and potash mined deep beneath the moors and also Teesside are used in huge quantities by the chemical industry. Coal, the fossilised remains of swamps within the river estuary which in their turn were covered by shales, created the wealth of the coal barons of Tyneside and County Durham. Other mineral riches were the lead ores which infiltrated narrow faults and cracks within the limestones of the upper dales. Lead is no longer mined, but barytes (lead carbonate) and fluorspa (calcium fluoride) associated with lead deposits, are in great demand, the former as a drilling aid in North Sea oil exploration and the later as a flux to improve the quality of steel.

In all the geological history of Northumbria, probably the most dramatic and certainly the most visibly lasting activity was the creation of the Great Whin Sill. Dolerite, a form of basalt forced its way underground between horizontal layers of the then surface rocks over an area which extends from Upper Teessdale in the west, where it can often be seen sandwiched between layers of one-time adjoining limestone, to the Farne Islands in the east. It outcrops most dramatically at Cauldron Snout in Teesdale and as the north-facing foundation crags of Hadrian's Wall.

HISTORY

At the time of the Roman occupation, what eventually became Northern England and Southern Scotland was loosely held by the Brigantians in the south and a confederation of the Otadini, Selgovae and Novantae tribes to the north. As the Romans were unable to control the whole of Britain, the narrow neck of land between modern Newcastle and Carlisle was made into a military zone, eventually tightened by the building of Hadrian's Wall. With the breakdown of the Roman Empire, the Wall and its surrounds were abandoned and Northumbria gradually fell into a state of anarchy, the Dark Ages. Land-hungry Saxons and Vikings from across the

North Sea took advantage of this situation, but not without much bloodshed. After the Norman Conquest huge castles were built along the coast to repell the continued threat from across the sea and gradually some form of order prevailed. However, Northumbria remained under threat from Scotland and for centuries border battles and skirmishes were an every day affair. Settling old scores both real and imaginary, was an excuse for cattle thieving and pillage until a couple of centuries ago.

Christianity came early to the north. Missionary monks trained in Ireland were sent to Northumbria and from a base on Holy Island, and despite the constant threat of Viking attack, spread the Gospel throughout the north. Their Celtic form of Christianity, with its beautifully decorated manuscripts, was only abandoned in deferrence to the rule of Canterbury in the early Middle Ages, following a dispute over the method of dating Easter. Ruins and beautiful churches together with decorated manuscripts and a few items of Celtic and Saxon jewellery are the tangible relics of a breed of devoted pioneers.

Many of the pioneers of the Industrial Revolution came from the North-East. Coal in abundance had to be transported to markets all over the country and horse-drawn railways were soon replaced by steam locomotives. Ship building also grew to meet the demands of overseas markets and steel to build those ships was made from locally-mined iron ore. Inventors rose to meet the challenge of a growing economy, together with engineers who found more effi-cient methods of building bigger and bigger machines. Armaments manufacturers developed the means of creating and defending an empire which expanded around this economy. Fortunes were made by the exploitation of nature's resources and great dynasties were founded in Northumbria. Much of this early industry has either disappeared or altered beyond all recognition, but the heritage is preserved in museums and centres throughout the region.

HOW TO USE THIS GUIDE

The guide is split into five chapters covering the counties of North-umberland, Tyne and Wear, County Durham and Cleveland to-gether with a separate chapter devoted to Hadrian's Wall. Starting at Berwick-upon-Tweed, the guide moves southwards by splitting each county into logical geographic areas, which are not necessarily the administrative regions. Descriptions generally follow valleys downstream and a separate section is devoted to the Northumber-land National Park. The Tyne and Wear chapter covers its industrial archaeology, Newcastle, towns and industry on either bank of the

Tyne and also the coast. County Durham is followed eastwards along its dales with separate sections on Durham city, the industry of its coalfield and the coast. Chapter 5 on Cleveland covers the towns and industrial history of Teesside, its coastal towns and the northern escarpment of the North York Moors. The chapter devoted to Hadrian's Wall describes it in context with the Roman military zone of northern England and follows the Wall from east to west, moving by necessity out of Northumbria into Cumbria. In order to fit in with the general north-south flow of the guide and also because many of the Roman features overlap the central counties, this chapter is included between Tyne and Wear and County Durham.

Special features are highlighted by symbols at the side of the text. At the end of some chapters short walks suitable for all age groups and also car drives, are shown separately. Six figure Grid References are included to help identify smaller features, ie Ross Castle (National Trust property), a prehistoric fort about 7 miles south-east of Wooler would be pinpointed as NU081254.

Things to do in Northumbria are almost unlimited. Whether you explore the remote fastnesses of the Cheviot Hills, visit a stately home such as Cragside, discover the North's industrial heritage at Beamish, trace the rise of Christianity or simply enjoy the freedom of miles of open sandy beaches, the choice is yours. Walking is an ever popular occupation and can range from tough moorland hikes to guided walks from the National Park Visitor Centre at Once Brewed on Hadrian's Wall. River and reservoir fishing is by permit only, but many of the coastal resorts offer sea angling trips and beach casting is popular all along the coast. Bird watching can vary between studying the habits of migratory birds on, for example, Holy Island, or going out on one of the boats from Seahouses to see the unbelievably tame nesting birds and seal colonies of the Farne Islands. In marked contrast, forests to the west and the high moors are home to differing species of birds. Motoring can be a joy along the miles of quiet by-ways in Northumbria, but take care when driving on unfenced roads, for sheep do not have much idea of road safety!

Descriptions of walks are kept to the minimum and are intended to be used in conjunction with an Ordnance Survey map.

Accommodation is as varied as the visitor's demands, from campsites and youth hostels to homely and comfortable farmhouse bed and breakfast establishments, to guest houses and rural hotels. Up to date details of available accommodation may be obtained from the Northumbria Tourist Board and information centres whose addresses and telephone numbers are given in Further Information. Some information centres offer a 'Book a Bed' service.

1

NORTHUMBERLAND

The county of Northumberland has some of the wildest and most remote countryside in England. The largest of the Northumbrian counties, it is a complex mixture of high moorland, forest, unspoilt coastline, attractive towns and villages and has a history which echoes the struggle for supremacy before Scotland and England became united under one crown.

For the purpose of this guide, the county is divided into three sections. Starting in the north, the first section is the English side of the Tweed and the coast. The second is devoted to the Cheviot Hills, the National Park and the Border Forests. The third and final section covers the Tyne Valley west of Tyne and Wear. As Hadrian's Wall and the Roman military zone are covered by a separate chapter, only passing reference is made to those Roman features which lie within Northumberland (and of course those which can be found in Tyne and Wear). Where practical, and with the exception of the Tweed, descriptions follow valleys downstream and investigate features within easy access of roads through those valleys.

THE TWEED & NORTHUMBERLAND COAST

Once a 'shuttlecock' between nations, **Berwick-upon-Tweed**, England's most northerly town, sits at the mouth of the Tweed and astride the Great North Road, although the road's modern counterpart, the A1(T) now takes all except local traffic away from the town by a modern high level bridge to the west of the fourth of a series of bridges across the Tweed, the oldest of which dates from 1610.

With the creation of the bypass, heavy traffic no longer brings chaos to this busy market town and the best approach for a first-time visitor is from the south across the Royal Tweed Bridge. It leads directly into a market place which has a limited number of parking

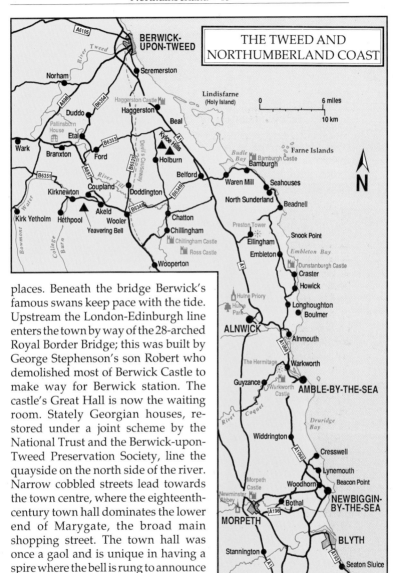

THE TWEED AND
NORTHUMBERLAND COAST

places. Beneath the bridge Berwick's famous swans keep pace with the tide. Upstream the London-Edinburgh line enters the town by way of the 28-arched Royal Border Bridge; this was built by George Stephenson's son Robert who demolished most of Berwick Castle to make way for Berwick station. The castle's Great Hall is now the waiting room. Stately Georgian houses, restored under a joint scheme by the National Trust and the Berwick-upon-Tweed Preservation Society, line the quayside on the north side of the river. Narrow cobbled streets lead towards the town centre, where the eighteenth-century town hall dominates the lower end of Marygate, the broad main shopping street. The town hall was once a gaol and is unique in having a spire where the bell is rung to announce services at the parish church of the Holy Trinity, a few streets away, which has no bell. This seventeenth-century church is one of the few built during the Commonwealth period after the Civil War, and has some remarkable stained glass.

Uphill along Marygate is the town wall where the gate is still a notorious bottleneck, but nothing like it was before the bypass was built. The walls are part of the Elizabethan ramparts, the ultimate in military architecture of the time and unique in Britain. Built between 1558 and 1566, they replaced earlier defences constructed around 1296 during the reign of Edward I. Traces of these earlier walls can still be seen around the town. The best way to explore Berwick and the river is by a circuit of the ramparts using a footpath along their crest. Guided tours, starting from Berwick Barracks, are organised from mid-March to mid-October.

Sir John Vanbrugh, architect of Blenheim Palace and Castle Howard, designed these barracks in 1717, after the first Jacobite uprising. Something of a showplace in its day, it became the home base of the King's Own Scottish Borderers but now houses a museum which tells the story of organised army life from Cromwellian times until the present day. Part of the Burrell Collection (the bulk of it is in Glasgow) is on display in the Clock Block of the Barracks.

The Tweed is a famous salmon river and the fish swim annually upstream to spawn in its headwaters. Commercial fishing is by net and is strictly controlled; sportsmen use elaborately tied flies and there are several specialist tackle shops around the town. Berwick has a deep sea fishing fleet and also a small boatyard. The dock and industrial area of the town is between Tweedmouth and Spittal on the south side of the river. There is an excellent sandy beach beyond Spittal.

The Border ceremony of Riding the Bounds, which has continued since the reign of Henry VII, takes place each year on 1 May. Horsemen follow Berwick's 10 mile boundary, with the mayor and civic party following by more sedate transport. The Tweed is the obvious border between England and Scotland and apart from a loop to the north of Berwick, the border follows the river as far as Carham between Coldstream and Kelso. A battle was fought on **Halidon Hill** in this loop to the north of Berwick on 19 July 1333. Access to the site is by public footpath from a car park near Camphill (NU976547) to the north of the A6105, about 3 miles north-west of Berwick-upon-Tweed. The 'Bendor' stone commemorating the battle can be found in the hedgerow alongside the A6105. There is a magnificent view from the top of Halidon Hill (535ft) which takes in Berwick-upon-Tweed and also the Cheviot Hills to the south-west.

Although there is a right-of-way, a fisherman's footpath, along the south (English) bank of the Tweed, the best way to explore it is by following the A698 and B6350 roads which run roughly parallel to the river and serve villages on the English side. The first village of note upstream along the Tweed is **Norham**, a pleasant Border village built high above the river and dominated by the ruins of its castle. Grey stone cottages fit snugly on either side of a wide village green where the cross stands on a medieval base. The main street leads towards a church founded by Eafrith, Bishop of Lindisfarne in 830. Originally a simple wooden structure, it was built to hold the remains of St Ceolwulf, the converted king to whom the Venerable Bede dedicated his ecclesiastical history of England. Norman Bishop Ranulph Flambard built the first stone church on this site. As Norham was constantly under the threat of attack by Scottish raiders from across the Tweed, the church was fortified. The present structure is the result of nineteenth-century modifications, but a number of Norman parts have survived, notably the chancel, its arch and the south arcade. The ruins of Norham Castle, now maintained by English Heritage, still command the river crossing and were built by Bishop Flambard in the twelfth century as part of the northern defences of the palatinate. Sir Walter Scott used Norham Castle as the setting for his Border noval *Marmion*, published in 1808.

The A698 continues south-west and passes one of the leading angling hotels along the border. Tillmouth Park is a country mansion, built in 1822 on the banks of the Till, a major tributary of the Tweed. The road crosses the Till by the single sweeping arch of Twizel Bridge. Built in 1450, it marks the turning point in the Battle of Flodden Field in 1513. On top of a high bank about 200yd downstream of the bridge, Twizel Castle's Norman-style ruins date only from the eighteenth century, but are in fact built on the site of an older fortification. A small deserted chapel nearby is said to be one of the places where St Cuthbert's body rested on its long journey around the North of England.

About 3 miles south-east of Cornhill-on-Tweed and to the south of the A697, the tiny village of **Branxton** marks the site of the Battle of Flodden Field (NU889373). This battle took place on 8 September 1513 when King James IV of Scotland and 9,000 of his followers were killed. It was the last and bloodiest battle to be fought in Northumbria. A simple service every August marks the tragedy.

Pallinburn House, an eighteenth-century mansion, is to the north of Branxton across a wide shallow valley; the walled and partly wild gardens are open to the public on advertised days, usually in spring when the displays of daffodils are at their best. About a mile along the A697 Coldstream road beyond the house, a 7ft-high standing stone, known as the King's Stone, is in a field on the right of the road. The B6350 now follows the river to **Wark-on-Tweed**, a

Berwick-upon-Tweed

tranquil village, but where a battle was fought in 1016 when the Scots under Malcolm II defeated an English army in open and bloody combat. It is also the site of a castle which in 1541 was described as 'a jewel of noysance' [nuisance] against the Scots who frequently, but without success laid seige. Founded in the twelfth century, the motte-and-bailey castle controlled an important river crossing.

The border leaves the Tweed beyond the tiny hamlet of Carham and turns roughly southwards across lush, gently rolling farmland, towards the highest summits of the Cheviot Hills. It crosses Bowmont Water, a fine trout and salmon river a mile or so north-east of **Kirk Yetholm**, traditional home of a gypsy clan and the Scottish end of the Pennine Way long distance footpath from Edale in Derbyshire. Following Bowmont Water downstream, the first village of note is **Kirknewton** at the foot of Yeavering Bell, an outlier of the Cheviot Hills. The compact village sits above the floodplain of the River Glen to the south-east of the confluence of College Burn and Bowmont Water. Thick stone cottage walls indicate their former need to withstand attack and the village still seems to crouch in on itself against Scottish raiders. Inside the church, a stone carving, thought to be Saxon, shows the Three Magi wearing kilts. The church is Early English and has a unique tunnel-vaulted chancel and south

Norham Castle keep

transept built on 3ft-high walls. Apart from the tower and nave, it appears to have escaped the zealous improvements of the eighteenth and nineteenth centuries. Josephine Butler, the Northumbrian social reformer, is buried in the churchyard.

College Burn valley is open to pedestrians beyond Hethpool and the farm track can be used as access to the Border Ridge, and also the Pennine Way. A hunt based on College Burn holds summertime competitions for riders and sportsmen, as well as sheepdog trials and terrier races, in a field beyond Hethpool close by the end of the public road. South-facing cultivation terraces on hillsides above Elsdon Burn, a tributary of College Burn, are the tangible remains of a civilisation which enjoyed a milder climate than today.

At **Old Yeavering** about a mile east of Kirknewton on the B6351 road to Wooler, a roadside stone indicates the site of the sixth century timber palace of the Anglo-Saxon kings of Northumbria. To its south, an Iron Age fort fills the summit of Yeavering Bell, marking the contrast between the two cultures. **Coupland Castle** is on the opposite bank of the River Glen. A private residence dating from the Union of Crowns, its grounds are open on advertised days.

River Glen turns north beyond Akeld, the village marking the junction of the B6351 and A697, to join the River Till. Before following the Till upstream past Wooler a diversion includes three interesting villages to the east of the A697. Follow this road for $4^1/_2$ miles and turn right along the B6354, then right again for a little way along the B6353 to reach **Ford** above the east bank of the Till. Here is an estate village of red-roofed cottages, built in the mid-1800s for Louisa, Marchioness of Waterford. She was an accomplished artist, a follower of the pre-Raphaelite Brotherhood, and who decorated the schoolhouse with frescoes of biblical themes using villagers and their children as her models. The building now known as Lady Waterford Hall, is open to the public throughout the year.

Lady Waterford lived above the village at Ford Castle, which dates from 1338. The present castle is a Victorian adaptation by Lady Waterford of the original quadrangular style. Thirteenth-century St Michael's Church in the castle grounds has an interesting bell tower.

Heatherslaw Mill about a mile north of Ford along the B6354 is a nineteenth-century flourmill operated by a massive under-shot waterwheel, which operates subject to water conditions. The mill is open to the public, together with a craft shop and café.

Etal further along the B6354, is a charming model village of whitewashed cottages lining a picturesque street which leads down to a ford across the Till. The castle ruins date from 1497 when it was last attacked by James IV. The garden of eighteenth-century Etal Manor is open on advertised days. A woodland garden with rhododendrons and flowering shrubs is at its best in May and June, and also September and October. The Black Bull, Northumberland's only thatched inn, is in the main street and a working smithy stands nearby.

About 2 miles further, the B6354 Berwick-upon-Tweed road makes a sharp bend at **Duddo**, a tiny agricultural village which fits around a junction with a minor road to Coldstream. A ruined sixteenth-century tower beyond a belt of trees opposite the village was once a watchtower against Scottish raiders.

Return by the A697 towards Wooler and pass the site of the Battle of Hamildon Hill (NU969295), which was fought in 1402. The road once echoed to the lowing of highland cattle on the long droves to

English markets. **Wooler**, a small market town, is the centre of a large farming community, where cattle fairs were held before rail, then road transport eased the movement of animals. The town has no buildings of great age, as it was destroyed by fire in 1722 and again in 1862. People have lived around Wooler for thousands of years: prehistoric settlements on nearby Harehope Hill (NU956285) and Earle Whin (NU985273), are testimony to long dead lifestyles. Wooler makes a good base for exploring the Cheviot Hills. Much of the history of the town and the surrounding district is explained in a permanent display at the Cheviot Field Centre and Museum in Padgepool Place.

Wooler Water, which once drove the town's mills, drains off the south-eastern face of The Cheviot. Minor roads give access to Happy Valley (NU997248), a delightful picnic spot, or past the oddly named Skirl Naked hillside and into the valley of Harthope Burn, the start of several footpaths climbing the eastern side of the Cheviots.

Doddington is to the north of Wooler, about 3 miles along the B6525. It sits above the floodplain of the River Till and is protected from easterly winds by Doddington Moor. The moor is the site of several interesting prehistoric earthworks and enigmatic 'cup and ring' carvings which are accessible from public footpaths. The thirteenth-century church of Saints Mary and Michael is unique, for its altar is situated at the west end.

Moving up the Till past **Chatton**, an estate village of mellow stone houses around a village green and with a Norman church 'beautified' in the late nineteenth century, a side road leads south to **Chillingham Castle**. Originally a small peel tower (peel, or pele towers, an important feature in Northumbria, were used as defence for both people and farm animals against border raiders), it was first developed as a fortress in the fourteenth century. The castle is basically four massive corner towers dominating the main wings which surround a central courtyard, and it is slowly being restored by a dedicated team. Of special note is the Italianate Garden, which was one of the first features to be brought back to its former glory. Chillingham is probably best known for its herd of wild white cattle. Claimed to be the purest surviving herd of native British cattle, the breed has remained unchanged since the Bronze Age. It is thought that the herd was trapped inside the 365 acres of parkland when it was enclosed in the thirteenth century. Visits to view the wild cattle are arranged in the company of the keeper throughout the summer. Dogs are not allowed on visits to the cattle, or in any part of the 260 acres of wild woodland surrounding the area used by the cattle. The tiny Norman estate church nearby is beautiful in its simplicity.

To the south of Chillingham Park and at the side of the minor road which climbs east across Hepburn Moor, are the remains of a 'bastle' (NU071249). These buildings are unique to the Cheviot region of Northumberland. They first appeared in the mid-sixteenth century and were a secure farmhouse built in stone to a standard design, in which the stock was kept on the windowless ground floor and humans lived above. Access to the upper floor and its arrow-slit windows was by an outside staircase. Many examples still survive, either as ruined barns, or incorporated into other buildings.

On top of the moorland escarpment above Chillingham Park is **Ross Castle** (NU081254), an Iron Age fort owned by the National Trust. It has one of the finest views in the district, ranging from the

Lady Waterford Hall, Ford

Cheviot Hills in the west to Bamburgh Castle, Lindisfarne and the Farne Islands in the east. Access is by a short footpath from the unfenced road across Hepburn Moor.

Continuing upstream to complete the northern and inland section of Northumberland, the Till now becomes the River Breamish and its headwaters are described in the section of this chapter devoted to the Northumberland National Park. An information board in a layby at the side of the A697 near **Wooperton**, about $6^1/_2$ miles south of

Wooler, marks the site of the Battle of Hedgeley Moor on 25 April 1464, a major skirmish in the Wars of the Roses, when a Lancastrian army was defeated by a Yorkist force. Two nearby stones, about 10yd apart, are known as Percy's Leap and are supposed to mark the gap across which the horse of Sir Ralph Percy, Earl of Northumberland, jumped when its rider was killed. The battle is also commemorated by the fifteenth-century Percy Cross, which stands by the side of the road a little further south along the road.

With the completion of this tour of the Tweed and its tributaries, attention is now turned northwards towards the coast. There are three routes from Wooler. The most obvious is the B6525, Wooler to Berwick-upon-Tweed road, but two unclassified roads to the east are quieter. To reach them it is necessary to travel north-east from Wooler along the B6349 towards Belford and turn north along either side of Hetton Burn. The most westerly road follows part of the Devil's Causeway, a Roman Road which ran north from *Corstopitum* (Corbridge) and crossed the Tweed at the site of Berwick-upon-Tweed. Both roads run through an area dotted with ancient earthworks. Those on Doddington Moor have already been mentioned, and to the north-east across Hetton Burn, St Cuthbert's Cave (NU059352) is supposed to be one of the sites where the saint's body rested on its long journey from Lindisfarne to Durham. Owned by the National Trust, the cave may be visited on a walk around Greensheen Hill above the little village of Holburn. To the north of the village, the Kyloe Hills, a mass of fell sandstone deposited by a primeval river, are mostly covered by forest, but their highest point and a craggy escarpment to the north are heather moors with wide views of the coast on either side of Holy Island.

The Coast

Travel south from Berwick-upon-Tweed along the A1(T), the Great North Road linking Scotland and London. Cosy inns in many of the villages are a pleasant reminder of the great days of coaching. The first village south of Berwick is **Scremerston**, where the Miners' Arms public house is the only link with a defunct coal mine, which once supported the village. The coastal nature reserve at Far Skerr (NU035480), can be reached by way of a minor road through the hamlet of Borewell Farm. Saltpan Rocks, between the reserve and Borewell Farm, are probably where salt was made by evaporating sea water. **Haggerston** about 5 miles down the road, is a small village with a caravan site surrounding a lake and a peel tower, the remains of a castle built in 1345.

A signpost at West Mains points the way over a level crossing and through Beal to **Holy Island**, or **Lindisfarne** to give it its older and more romantic sounding name. To reach the island it is necessary to drive over a causeway which is only open at low tide. *Never* attempt the crossing at other than authorised times; lives have been lost on these treacherous sands, and many motorists have spent an uncomfortable three or four hours stranded in the refuge tower through ignoring the tide tables posted on either side of the causeway.

Christianity was brought here by Celtic missionaries, but it was many years, years before St Aidan was able to establish a priory on Lindisfarne in 635. The island was comparatively safe from mainland attack, but prey to marauding Vikings in later years. A crude, but graphic stone carving in the priory museum conveys the terror of a Viking raid. St Cuthbert, the missionary, came to the island in 664. On his death in 687, he was buried on Lindisfarne, but 11 years later while waiting to move his tomb to a more honoured site, the monks decided to disinter his body. On opening the coffin, it was found to be still intact and the saint appeared to be simply asleep. From that time onwards his remains became a sacred relic and when an increase in Viking raids caused the monks to flee the island in 875, they took his still-intact body with them. They moved around the North of England for over a hundred years, never able to settle for long in any one place, until a devine revelation instructed the monks to take St Cuthbert's remains to Dunholm. The site later became the magnificent cathedral city of Durham.

Most of the work of developing the priory took place under St Cuthbert's successor, St Wilfrid. It was during his reign that many wonderful works of art were made, such as St Cuthbert's Cross, which is now in Durham Cathedral, and the exquisitely decorated Lindisfarne Gospels, which can be seen in the British Museum in London. A modern facsimile of the Gospels is in St Mary's, the priory church, the only building left intact after Henry VIII's edict led to the dissolution of the priory. Lindisfarne is still a place of pilgrimage, and St Cuthbert is the patron saint of Northumberland.

The sole village on the island uses Holy Island as its name. Originally the priory's service village, its inhabitants are now mostly fishermen, or employees in the handful of pleasant pubs and hotels catering for visitors. A market cross in the tiny square dates from 1828, but rises from a medieval socket. The island's only farm uses the ample grazing on Chare Ends, between the dunes to the north and Lindisfarne Castle in the south.

Most of the long eastern, dune-covered arm of Holy Island is a bird sanctuary and nature reserve. It is possible to walk round the island's foreshore, but dogs should be under close control at all times. The removal of birds' eggs and plants is illegal.

The Whin Sill, the vast extrusion of doleritic basalt that appears throughout Northern England in places as far apart as Teesdale, Hadrian's Wall and the Farne Islands, has created the highest point of Holy Island. Lindisfarne Castle sits on top of rocky Beblowe Crag and was built as part of a coastal defence scheme in 1550. Occupied by Parliamentary troops during the Civil War, it eventually fell into disrepair, but was transformed in 1903 into a magnificent house for Edward Hudson, the publisher of *Country Life*, by the architect Sir Edwin Lutyens. The castle and its fine collection of oak furniture is open to the public. It was given to the National Trust in 1944 by Sir Edward de Stein and his sister Miss Gladys de Stein. The Trust also own the surrounding 30 acres of land, together with the tiny walled garden nearby. Sheltered from winds off the North Sea, it was created by the landscape gardener Gertrude Jekyll between 1906 and 1912. From Castle Point on Holy Island, the view across the wide inlet is one of miles of sand dunes topped by a glimpse of Bamburgh Castle in the distance.

Back on the mainland, **Belford** was a busier place when mail coaches trundled along the Great North Road, but only the ivy-covered Blue Bell Inn remains from this time. The inn faces a simple market cross and in side streets agricultural suppliers' offices indicate the village's present-day importance as a marketplace for the surrounding farmland. Belford Hall was built in 1756 to a design by James Paine. After several years of neglect, it has now been tastefully reconstructed by the Northern Heritage Trust.

The B1342 from Belford reaches the sea at **Budle Bay**, an esturial nature reserve surrounded by sand dunes. Access is from **Waren Mill**, once an important sea port. The harbour has long since disappeared, silted up beneath the sands of the estuary. Spindlestone Heugh (pronounced 'heeuff'), the small hill beyond the campsite, features in the Northumbrian ballad of the *Laidly Worm*.

Bamburgh village sits snugly beneath the protection of its massive sandstone castle and has a somewhat medieval atmosphere. Pleasant low stone houses line its two main streets and the village huddles behind a natural rocky barrier and sand dunes, protected from harsh north-easterly winds blowing off the North Sea.

Grace Darling, heroine of the brave rescue of survivors of the wreck of the SS *Forfarshire* which ran aground on the Farne Islands in 1838, was born in the village. The Grace Darling Museum opposite the church commemorates her life and the rescue. St Aidan's church, where she is buried, is a mid-seventh-century foundation, but the present building is thirteenth century with Victorian alterations.

Lindisfarne Priory

Lindisfarne Castle

Bamburgh Castle is dramatically set on its high rock and is a landmark for miles along the Northumbrian coast. Its present romantic appearance is largely the result of restoration: some in the eighteenth century, but more by the first Lord Armstrong, the engineer and armaments king, who paid for the last and most ambitious work. Viewed from the village, the castle fills the whole of the upper crag on which it sits, an outcrop of the Great Whin Sill. It is open to the public from Easter to October.

Sand dunes restrict any seaward views from the B1340 until it reaches **Seahouses**. This holiday village and inshore fishing port did not exist until 1889 when the harbour was built in order to improve the local fishing industry. Amenities include a yachting and skin-diving centre, good beaches on either side of the headland and a well-varied shopping centre which includes several shops selling fish landed in the harbour and excellent locally smoked kippers. Close by the harbour is a maritime museum and an information centre. Now linked to Seahouses, the older village of **North Sunderland** became something of a backwater when the harbour was built, but it contains some attractive stone cottages.

Visitors embark for the **Farne Islands** from Seahouses' harbour. This group of basaltic islands and rocks, the final outliers of the Great

Whin Sill, lie between 2 and 5 miles offshore to the north of Seahouses. Owned by the National Trust, the islands are divided into two main groups, the Inner and Outer Farnes; their actual number varies according to the state of the tide. The largest, which gives its name to the group is Farne Island. It has a lighthouse built near an ancient tower where a coal-fired beacon once warned shipping. Above the slipway, a fourteenth-century chapel on the site of St Cuthbert's Hermitage has been a place of pilgrimage for centuries.

Probably the best-documented shipwreck on the Farne Islands was that of the ill-fated SS *Forfarshire*. Drifting in a violent storm on the night of 7 September 1838, and with its engines out of commission, the vessel struck Harcar Rocks. At that time the lighthouse on Longstone was manned by Grace Darling and her father. Despite the ferocity of the storm, they rowed out to the *Forfarshire* and after many difficult journeys managed to rescue a number of passengers and crew.

The first inhabitant of the Farne Islands was St Aidan, Bishop of Lindisfarne from 635 to 651. He built a simple stone cell on Farne Island to pray and mediate in peace. His successor was St Cuthbert, who made the island his home from 676 to 685. He befriended the nesting birds and eider ducks are still known locally as 'St Cuthbert's chicks'. For centuries, the Farnes were an easy source of eggs and as a result the bird population had declined alarmingly by the late 1800s. The Farne Islands Association was formed in 1880 to protect the wildlife of the island and in 1925 the National Trust acquired the islands with the exception of the Longstone lighthouse. In 1964, the islands became a bird sanctuary. Regular sailings from Seahouses visit the islands and during the cruise around the outer group, seals can be seen basking on the rocks of Longstone. Visitors can usually land on Farne Island where they must run the gauntlet of overprotective kittiwakes which 'dive bomb' the approach to the nesting area. Once past their attentions, the nesting birds are so tame that close-up photography is an easy matter. Birdwatching and botanical visits can be arranged via the National Trust Warden, c/o The Shieling, 8 St Aidan's, Seahouses, ☎ Seahouses (066 572) 651 (see Further Information).

A couple of miles down the coast is the holiday resort of **Beadnell**, rather dominated by a caravan site, and many of its houses second homes; but the rocky foreshore and sandy beach more than compensate for this. The small harbour is overlooked by eighteenth-century lime kilns, now cared for by the National Trust. The village church is Victorian Gothic, and the remains of St Ebbe's chapel also overlook the harbour. A pleasant eighteenth-century inn, the Craster

Arms, is in the main street and a fifteenth-century peel tower stands to the west of the village. An unspoilt sandy beach leads to Newton Links above Snook Point, a little over a mile to the south of Beadnell; here there are 55 acres of sand dunes owned by the National Trust. A pleasant 5-6 mile walk can be enjoyed by walking along the beach at low tide as far as Snook Point or beyond, and returning by the footpath behind the dunes.

The dramatic and isolated ruins of **Dunstanburgh Castle** (NU257218) stand on an 11-acre rocky headland to the south of Embleton Bay. The artist J.M.W. Turner painted the ruins, capturing the North Sea scene in evening light. Sea birds nest on the cliffs below the castle and also in the dunes further inland. Dunstanburgh, under the guardianship of English Heritage, is a National Trust property, as are Embleton Links — 214 acres of dunes and foreshore — together with the tiny fishing village of Low Newton-by-the-Sea and Newton Links, 55 acres of dunes to its north. Freshwater Newton Pool to the south of the village, also a National Trust property, is of special ornithological significance, attracting visiting migrant birds from the Arctic and Siberia as well as northern Europe. There is no road access to the castle; the best approach is by the easy $1^1/_2$ mile seashore footpath north of Craster, or by a slightly longer path around Embleton Bay, which starts near the Embleton Bay Golf Course club house.

A signposted minor road off the B1339 leads to **Craster**. This pleasant fishing village, famous for its oak-smoked kippers, does not reveal itself until the last possible moment. An outcrop of the Whin Sill blocks the view; once quarried, the dolerite based rock was shipped from the tiny stone-jettied harbour. The Arnold Memorial Trail winds around the quarried crags to show the geological formations and also visits nearby woodlands. Small sandy beaches sheltered by outcropping rocks line and a coastline much favoured by sea birds.

Howick Hall, a private house on the winding road between Craster and Longhoughton, was built in 1782 on the site of a fifteenth-century tower. The gardens are open to the public from April to September, although the best time to visit is in May and June, when the rhododendrons are in full bloom.

A mock ruined castle stands on Ratcleugh Crag near **Longhoughton**. The church was founded in Norman times, but the present structure is mostly Victorian, although an original arch was left unaltered. The tower was used as a place of safety from border raiders.

An unclassified side road leads to the coast where the small

Fishing boat at Seahouses

Craster harbour →

An Arctic tern one of a number of birds which nest on Farne Island

Sea stacks crowned in white

village of **Boulmer** was once the haunt of smugglers. Only a few single-storied fishermen's cottages remain from what was once a busy fishing village. Today's fishermen are mostly engaged in inshore fishing for lobsters, crabs and sea salmon, and they still use the traditional East Coast coble (pronounced 'cobble'), a beach boat with a transom stern which owes its ancestry to the Viking longboat. Boulmer has no harbour and craft must be hauled ashore. Sandy beaches alternate with a rocky foreshore on either side of Boulmer, the haunt of sea birds.

Moving inland again, **Alnwick** (pronounced 'Annick') is no longer troubled by through traffic along the A1, which now by-passes it along a broad embankment to the east. Alnwick is the major town in this central part of Northumberland; strategically placed at a crossing of the river Aln, the town grew beneath the guardian walls of its castle. Narrow winding streets and an intimate market square still evoke an atmosphere of the medieval past, a past which is re-enacted each year during the costumed Alnwick Fair. Alnwick has been an important commercial centre since its first market charter in 1291. In a corner of the market place the stepped market cross looks out on to the Northumberland Hall, an imposing building erected in 1826. To one side is the older town hall, dating from 1771. Beyond the square are the Shambles, where butchers' shops stood in medieval times. The parish church of St Michael is mostly Perpendicular in style and dates from the fourteenth century, probably replacing a Norman building on the same site.

Many of Alnwick's inns, notably the Nag's Head, have catered for travellers since the sixteenth century, and more especially when the Great North Road, the predecessor of the A1(T) came through Alnwick. Old Cross Inn in Narrowgate is better known as 'Dirty Bottles', from a row of bottles which have remained untouched in a bow window for almost 200 years. A local superstition believes that anyone removing them will die.

Although **Alnwick Castle** dates from the eleventh century, the present building is the result of careful restoration in the eighteenth century, with internal alterations in the Victorian era by Anthony Salvin for the fourth Duke of Northumberland. The castle is still the home of the present duke, who lives under the protection of warlike statues lining the battlements, carved by James Johnson in the mid-1800s. The castle is open to the public at advertised times from May to October and the interior is richly decorated in the Classical style, together with paintings by Canaletto, Van Dyck and Titian. There are also dungeons, an armoury and an interesting museum of local remains dating from pre-Roman times; the Royal Northumberland

Fusiliers Regimental Museum is housed in the Abbot's Tower. The park was landscaped by 'Capability' Brown and stretches away to the north across the River Aln; the best view of the park is from the castle terrace.

Visitors arriving by road from the south cannot fail to notice the 83ft tall tower at the roadside near the hospital. Surmounted by a lion with its tail stiffly out-stretched, it is the symbol of the Percy's, the Dukes of Northumberland. Rising from a base of five other lions, the tower was built in 1816 as a gift from ducal tennants to thank him for reducing their rents following a drop in food prices at the end of the Napoleonic Wars. Percy lions feature in Turner's painting of Alnwick Castle viewed in moonlight from the bridge.

Modern Alnwick is the commercial centre for a rich agricultural region and its industries are mostly connected with farming. It also makes fishing tackle and distils rum. The House of Hardy fishing tackle company, whose founder perfected the method of joining split canes together to make strong yet supple fly rods, have a factory at Willowburn on the outskirts of the town which is open to the public from March to October.

Parkland fills the northern approach to Alnwick. **Abbeylands** is part of the castle park, with the scant riverside remains of Alnwick Abbey, founded by monks of the Premonstratensian order. Upstream, Hulne Park stretches on either side of the Aln and here are the remains of Hulne Priory, a fortified abbey founded by the carmelite order of White Friars in 1240. Although very much reduced in size, a considerable portion of the site is well preserved. The massive curtain wall is complete, although most of its defences are gone, except Lord's Tower; this was added in 1488. After the Dissolution, the priory became something of a pleasure garden for later Percys and the first Duke added a pseudo-Gothic summerhouse in 1777. The priory church remains and, in keeping with the Carmelite order, is aisleless; it is also a mixture of styles from medieval to Victorian. From the priory; a $1^3/_4$ mile riverside and forest walk leads upstream to Brizlee Tower, another pseudo-Gothic ornamentation, built for the first Duke by Robert Adam.

The River Aln meanders in tight bends across the narrow coastal plain, and at the mouth of the river, **Alnmouth** is an unspoilt seaside village on a south-facing peninsula. Its roots are ancient and go back to the earliest days of Christianity in the North-East; a sculptured shaft of an eighth-century cross found nearby is now in Alnwick Castle Museum. Alnmouth was an important seaport in medieval times, and today its harbour is a popular anchorage for pleasure craft and inshore fishing boats. Sandy beaches and sheltered rocky havens stretch along the coast to the north and south of the estuary. The village has a 9-hole golf course; Foxton Hall, to the north, is a championship course.

The A1068 roughly follows the dune-lined coast to **Warkworth**. A modern bridge carries the road across the Coquet, but does not detract in any way from the beauty of its medieval predecessor, a few yards upstream. The twin-arched bridge and its stone guard-house is open only to pedestrians and makes the best entry into this ancient fortified town. Warkworth is built on a rocky spur and mellow stone properties line Castle Street, which climbs by way of the market

Old Cross Inn, Alnwick

square to the still dominant castle. The parish church of St Laurence, a fine example of Norman architecture is reputed to be built on eighth-century foundations; it has a spire, a rarity in Northumberland, erected in the fourteenth century. A mile-long pathway upstream from the village, leads to the Hermitage (an English Heritage property), a hermit's cell carved from the sandstone cliff. In use until the sixteenth century, it has a vaulted ceiling and scenes of the Passion carved into the rock.

Warkworth Castle dates from the twelfth century, but its stone-framed windows speak of habitation in more settled times. The Percys, who once used it as their home, were responsible for the improvements, which were designed by Anthony Salvin in the nineteenth century. A tall slender central watchtower looks out over the surrounding plain and the sea, still guarding against long vanished enemies. The castle is maintained by English Heritage. There is a golf course to the north-east of Warkworth, and a clean sandy beach together with a well appointed caravan park.

A little over a mile downstream, the Coquet widens at its estuary

Warkworth Castle, overlooking River Coquet

to form Warkworth Harbour, a haven for pleasure craft and inshore fishing boats. The small seaport of **Amble** is on the south side of the river mouth, where coal from the northern edge of the Northumbrian coalfield is still exported. Some of the local seams are close enough to the surface for coal to be washed ashore during winter gales, providing free fuel for anyone hardy enough to brave the elements. **Coquet Island** is about a mile offshore. The haunt of eider duck and other sea birds, it has the foundations of a tiny twelfth-century Benedictine monastery. Now guarded by a lighthouse, the island, which is directly in line with the harbour entrance, was once a notorious hazard to shipping.

Moving upstream along the winding tree-lined River Coquet, **Guyzance,** at the junction of a series of narrow lanes between the A1 and the B6345, faces south, high above the north bank of the river. Guyzance Hall is famous for its rose gardens and herbaceous borders, and is open on advertised days. The ruins of an ancient priory and St Wilfrid's Chapel lie across the river to the south-west of this attractive farming community. John Smeaton, the eighteenth-century engineer, almost ruined the salmon fishing on the Coquet when he built a weir to control the river's flow, but a salmon ladder now eases their way upstream.

South of Amble, the 7-mile sweep of unspoilt sandy beach facing **Druridge Bay** runs unimpeded to Cresswell where 99 acres of sand dunes and grass hinterland were bought by the National Trust in 1972 with funds provided by Enterprise Neptune. **Cresswell** marks the end of Druridge Bay and the foreshore to its south is mostly rocky. There is a spacious village green where Cresswell Tower, a fourteenth-century fortified dwelling, stands above a tunnel-vaulted ground floor. The village church is neo-Norman, built in 1836, and contains some interesting stained glass. Industrial Northumberland commands the coast southwards, mostly based on locally mined coal and limestone. **Lynemouth** is a little inland from the mouth of its river; a compact industrial town of carefully laid out streets, focusing on its Miners' Institute. The River Lyne loops tightly around the town from west to north, flowing through an attractively wooded dene which has a $1^1/_4$ mile footpath linking Lynemouth to the nearby village of Ellington. Fosslized tree stumps sometimes appear on the sandy beach after winter storms.

A power station linked to its own colliery and the Lynemouth aluminium works are separated from **Newbiggin-by-the-Sea** by a golf course in the dunes behind Beacon Point. The town seems to turn its back on the sea and concentrates on providing homes for aluminium workers and miners who work in the pits further inland, but there is no longer a mine at Newbiggin. The seaward side of the town is a pleasant sandy bay with holiday and camping amenities. St Bartholomew's Church sits on a headland outside the town and is basically of the thirteenth and fourteenth centuries. Its ancient tower still acts as a landmark for shipping, but the interior is modern. Erosion is a constant threat along this part of the coast and the church is in danger of eventually falling into the sea. About a mile outside Newbiggin, along the A197 Morpeth road, **Woodhorn** church stands beside a little wood. Although it looks very much a Victorian structure, it is built on Saxon and Norman foundations with some Early English additions. Redundant since its parishioners moved away following the closure of local pits, the building is now used as a museum and cultural centre. **Wansbeck Riverside Park** is set along a 2-mile, partly wooded stretch of the tidal Wansbeck. Waterside facilities include picnic sites, sailing, river fishing and a caravan site.

Upstream and on a minor road linking the A1068 and A196, the model village of **Bothal** is at the end of a spur between the wooded denes of Brock's Burn and the River Wansbeck. The tiny village is centered on its Saxon church and also the ruins of Bothal Castle, which was built in 1343. The wooded denes of the Wansbeck and Brock's Burn are accessible by a $4^1/_2$ mile riverside footpath between Pegswood and Morpeth, or from a short path below the castle.

The A1(T) bypasses **Morpeth**, but inns in the centre of the town still have their coach yards, links with a time when Morpeth was an important stopping place on the Great North Road. Telford built the town bridge in 1831, part of a big improvement scheme for the main road between London and Edinburgh. Modern shop fronts hide the splendid architecture of Georgian buildings in the main street, but Morpeth's spacious tree-lined boulevards still manage to convey the more leisurely aspect of travel in a bygone age. Modern Morpeth has become the main town of Castle Morpeth Borough and also the county town of Northumberland, as well as being a busy market centre for the surrounding countryside. The town, which straddles the River Wansbeck, once lived under the protection of a castle, but its only remains are the fifteenth-century gatehouse and a motte and bailey on a steep slope above the river in Carlisle Park. Castle Square is situated at the southern end of Telford's bridge and to its east is the massive Court House, a late Georgian building designed by John Dobson, the Newcastle architect.

St Mary's Parish Church is mostly fourteenth century, but is built on Norman foundations. Following a delightful local custom, the church gates are tied after weddings until the bridegroom pays a toll. A watchtower next to the churchyard was built in 1837 to guard against bodysnatchers, and a nearby secular clock tower, one of only eight in Britain, still tolls a curfew bell.

About three quarters of a mile to the west of the town centre, and reached by an attractive riverside footpath, are the ruins of **Newminster Abbey**, a Cistercian foundation dating from 1137. Ravaged by the Scots soon after its initial completion, the rebuilt abbey became extremely powerful until the Dissolution edict of Henry VIII.

Morpeth has two museums; the Cameo Gallery in King Edward VI School, which holds temporary exhibitions in conjunction with lectures on a wide range of subjects, and on the north side of Telford's Bridge the Chantry, which dates from 1296, an eloquent reminder of Morpeth's past. The latter building holds a collection of Northumbrian Small Pipes (the local version of bagpipes), as well as housing a craft centre, and it is also used as a tourist information centre.

About $1^1/_2$ miles south-west of Bedlington, **Plessey Woods Country Park** follows a wooded dene along the banks of the Blyth.

Woodland and riverside walks are aided by interpretive displays of the natural history of the area.

The pleasant village of **Stannington** is built mainly to the west of the A1 about 4 miles south of Morpeth. The village stands on gentle slopes above a side stream to the north of the River Blyth. Its church tower rises above the wooded valley and makes a landmark for travellers along the Great North Road. An attractive $2^1/_2$ mile riverside and woodland walk through Stannington Vale leads along the north bank of the Blyth from Stannington Bridge, eastwards into Plessey Woods Country Park.

Blagdon Hall is $1^1/_2$ miles south of Stannington. The house was built in 1735, but has been altered over the years, most recently by Sir Edwin Lutyens, who also designed the present gardens. The house is privately owned, but the gardens and parkland are open on advertised days.

Back on the coast, **Blyth** takes its name from the river; the town spreads to the south along the estuary and in keeping with its industrial day-to-day affairs, mainly turns its back on the sea. The oldest part of the town is built around Northumberland Street and nearby is an eighteenth-century lighthouse, standing a little incongruously inland behind some terraced houses. South of the town and well away from industry, are sandy beaches, and a golf course, while camping and caravan sites on the foreshore beyond the Nautical School give this part of the town a holiday resort atmosphere.

Despite the occasional sprawl of bungalows and modern housing estates inland, **Seaton Sluice** remains a pretty seaside town; its red-roofed cottages have appeared on many an artist's canvas. The finest building in the town centre is the Octagon, attributed to Vanbrugh, the designer of Castle Howard.

Strictly part of Tyne and Wear, but reached by a pleasant mile-long cliff top path from Seaton Sluice, the offshore island of **St Mary's** or **Bait Island** is connected to the mainland by a short tidal causeway. The 126ft-high lighthouse, erected in 1897-8, stands on the site of a monastic cell where traditionally the sanctuary light once acted as a guide for inshore vessels. The lighthouse is no longer manned, but still acts as a navigational aid. Sea birds nest on the island and grey seals are frequent visitors; its rocks make an excellent vantage point for sea angling. There is a small car park at the landward end of the causeway, which is reached along a side track leaving the A193 near the caravan park to the north of Whitley Bay.

There is a fine view of seventeenth-century **Seaton Delaval Hall** from the A190. The house is a masterwork of Sir John Vanbrugh, architect of many of the grand houses throughout the north. It was built in Palladian style, and huge Tuscan columns support the portico of the central block with ornate wings projecting on either side, one being the stables. A Norman church, developed as the family chapel but now used as the parish church, stands in the grounds. House and gardens are open on advertised days throughout the summer from May to September.

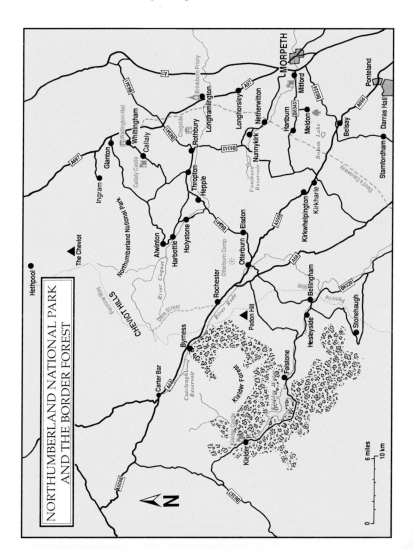

NORTHUMBERLAND NATIONAL PARK AND THE BORDER FOREST

NORTHUMBERLAND NATIONAL PARK AND THE BORDER FORESTS

England's most northerly national park stretches from the Cheviot Hills and the Scottish border in the north to Hadrian's Wall in the south, and covers a total of about 398sq miles. The Northumberland National Park, like all the other ten National Parks in England and Wales, does not own the land it covers; its main duties are to safeguard the landscape, set building standards compatible with existing architecture, and encourage the public to appreciate and enjoy this unique area of natural beauty. A full-time and part-time warden service has been formed to help visitors to enjoy the countryside and also prevent any conflict of interests.

Although the Northumberland National Park has one of the lowest populations of any national park in England and Wales, three man-made features dominate its boundaries, the largest being the Forestry Commission's Border Forests, which spread west from within the park. Another is Kielder Water, Europe's largest reservoir. Visitor amenities have been created in both features by the co-operation of the Forestry Commission, Northumbrian Water and the National Park. The final and most ancient feature is Hadrian's Wall, which crosses the narrowest part of England, from Newcastle upon Tyne in the east to the Solway Firth beyond Carlisle in the west. The best preserved and scenically most attractive portions of the Wall lie within the park. Once Brewed Information Centre is on the B6318, $3^1/_2$ miles north-west of Haltwistle; provided by the Northumberland National Park it acts as an interpretive centre for Hadrian's Wall, as well as giving local and other information about activities within the park. Housesteads Roman Fort Information Centre, further along the B6318, is jointly run by the National Park and the National Trust.

Many of the high moors to the south-west of the Cheviot Hills are used by the military for training and while there are rights-of-way routes across the ranges, they *must not be entered while the red warning flags are flying.* Anyone walking on footpaths through the ranges should take care not to touch any suspicious objects left lying around. Roadside parking and picnic sites have been created on many of the scenically interesting roads in the area. The Forestry Commission's 12 miles of Forest Drive (a toll road) is between Kielder and the A68, with picnic sites and waymarked forest walks.

The Pennine Way long distance footpath traverses the park on its way north to Scotland and miles of right-of-way footpaths criss-cross the moors and fells in the rest of the region. In the north, the Cheviot

Hills offer challenging walks for the more experienced, but easier paths can be found in the south of the park. Organized walks, often with intetpretive themes, are led by competent guides throughout the summer months, and to a lesser extent in winter. Details of the walks and other events are given on the *Discovery Walks and Trails* leaflet, available from information centres and local libraries or direct from the National Park Office. Many facilities and amenities in and around the park are accessible to the disabled: see the Northumberland National Park leaflet *A Disabled Visitor's Guide*.

Local rock-climbing areas can be found on the dolerite of the Whin Sill escarpment around Crag Lough and also in the Simonside Hills near Rothbury. Access is not always available and it is usual to ask permission from the local landowners.

Horse riding and pony trekking from local stables are both popular in the park; the wide and open nature of the countryside makes it ideal for these activities. Up-to-date lists of stables and pony trekking establishments are available from the National Park Authority, or Tynedale District Council.

Most of the rivers and reservoirs within the National Park are privately owned, but many angling clubs sell day tickets and Kielder Reservoir has been stocked with trout and other fish. Rod licences are available from Northumbrian Water.

A bus service from Hexham to Haltwhistle by way of Hadrian's Wall operates Monday to Saturday from the end of July to the end of August. Frequent stopping places make it easy to explore sections of the Wall and surrounding countryside without the need to return on foot to the starting point.

Five major rivers start their life in the Northumberland National Park; two, College Burn and the River Breamish respectively drain the north and south sides of The Cheviot, 2,676ft (816m), the highest and perhaps boggiest place in the park. Both rivers are tributaries of the Tweed. The River Coquet flows unimpeded, all the way to reach the North Sea at Amble, but both the Rede and Warksburn are tributaries of the North Tyne.

The following paragraphs give details of the villages and major features within the park. As there is a separate chapter devoted to Hadrian's Wall, only passing reference to Roman sites will be made here.

North and East Flowing Valleys

The lower part of College Burn has already been described earlier in this chapter. A 5-mile valley-bottom track from Hethpool, closed to all except pedestrians and local traffic, gives access to the dalehead where a footpath climbs up to the border fence and the Pennine Way's last stage northwards. A path follows the border as far as an acute angle in the fence, then turns east through a series of peat hags and north-east for a mile across an extremely boggy moor to the summit of The Cheviot. Much more interesting is the Hen Hole (NT886203); this craggy ravine is to the east of the dalehead path and is the true source of College Burn. The rocks of Hen Hole are the weathered remains of an ancient volcano, one of several which flourished millions of years ago in what became the Borders.

Of all the rivers draining the Cheviot Hills, the Breamish in its upper reaches is undoubtedly the wildest. It rises on a remote moor south of The Cheviot and flows down a deep-cut valley until it reaches more level and fertile lands on either side of the A697 to the east. **Ingram** stands at the mouth of the narrowest part of the dale, a secluded cluster of stone cottages at the end of a side road off the A697 south of Wooler. The village fits snuggly above flood level on the south side of the river and at the foot of the east-facing slopes of Ewe Hill, an outlier of the Cheviot Hills. Ingram is a natural gateway to the moors and high tops of the Cheviots, and useful data about local conditions can be obtained from the National Park Information Centre in the village. Numerous hut circles and other prehistoric sites can be found on the nearby moors; most notable is the Graves Ash site (NT964163) near Linhope Farm at the end of the surfaced road towards the head of the Breamish valley. This is the largest complex in Northumberland and contains traces of at least forty huts, which were occupied from the Iron Age until Roman times. A medieval farmstead is superimposed upon the group.

Davidson's Linn (NT885157) is an attractive waterfall about 7 miles from Linhope, at the head of Usway Burn in the Coquet valley. It is only accessible by a lonely moorland path, once used by packhorses carrying salt into the Borders, climbing out of the Breamish valley beyond the remote High Bleakhope Farm. The walk, a total of 14 miles is only suitable in fine weather and could include an exploratory visit to the Greaves Ash site.

Although it is $3^1/_2$ miles outside the boundary of the National Park, **Glanton** is closely linked in character to the remote villages of the eastern side of the park. The quiet village stands at the junction of five minor roads, about 10 miles west of Alnwick and west of the A697 Morpeth to Coldstream road. It shelters beneath the south-eastern shoulder of Glanton Hill, an outlier of the Cheviots, and its elevated position commands extensive views across the Aln and Breamish valleys. The World Bird Research Station was opened at Glanton in 1930 for the study of wild bird life in the Border region. The station organizes the annual recording of dawn and dusk choruses throughout the British Isles and is open to visitors from June to mid-October.

Whittingham, about 2 miles to the south, is another village outside the National Park, but linked in character. The Aln divides the village in two; the northern half follows the river, and it is here that the church stands. Dating from Saxon times, it was over-zealously 'improved' during the reign of Queen Victoria. A peel tower opposite the church has been converted into almshouses. 'South' Whittingham is across the Aln, a pretty group of houses arranged around a village green. The village holds an annual Games Fair each August, a popular event for the surrounding area. The Whittingham Sword, one of a number of Bronze Age weapons discovered at Thrunton Farm to the south-east, is now on display in the Castle Museum, Newcastle.

Callalay Castle is on the winding road between Whittingham and Thropton, about 2 miles south-west of the former. An interesting building with a complex history, the present structure is basically a thirteenth-century peel tower which, with the easing of Border raids, was extended in 1676 and again in 1835. However, the tower itself stands on the site of a much older stronghold. Today the castle is a gracious home in a beautiful setting. The entrance hall, built in 1750, is sumptuously decorated in Italian style. The Georgian and Victorian interior of the rest of the building contains exquisite plasterwork and many notable items of furniture, as well as paintings by Hogarth and a Gobelin tapestry dated 1787. The house and its pleasant gardens are open from May to September.

Callalay Park was enclosed in 1704 and extends from the castle towards the slopes of Callalay Hill where there are traces of pre-historic settlements. Catholic priests were once hidden from persecution in an artificial cave on Callalay Hill.

The narrow winding road along the Coquet valley can claim to be one of the least frequented roads in England. Serving isolated sheep farms, it skirts the Otterburn Artillery Ranges before turning south-east into the ranges at the valley head near a group of Roman marching camps at Chew Green. This strange cluster of earthworks were a series of temporary camps, often superimposed on one another. Footpaths from the dalehead spread fan-wise to reach the Scottish border.

The remote village of **Alwinton** is the focal point of farms and hamlets in the upper Coquet valley and is about 9 miles north-west of Rothbury. It sits on a sunny plateau above the junction of the Coquet with the River Alwin. Being enclosed by high Cheviot moors on all sides gives the village a general air of tranquillity and makes it an ideal centre for walks in the central Cheviots, and for trout fishing in the local rivers. The village church was founded in the twelfth century, but was very much altered about 1851.

Clennel Street, a moorland track marked by enigmatic cairns and earthworks, climbs the steep hillside above Alwinton. In use long before the Romans made their way northwards, it was later followed by cattle drovers on the long march south.

A couple of miles downstream from Alwinton, **Harbottle's** light-brown cottages nestle beneath the scant remains of an ancient castle. There is another castle in Harbottle, to the east of the village, but this is a comparatively recent addition and was built in 1829 as a shooting lodge. It is now a private house and craft centre.

The Drake Stone is a rock near a small lake, about $1^1/_4$ miles uphill by a footpath to the west of Harbottle. It is considered locally to be misnamed: it should be 'Dragon Stone', and is a place where primitive rites are supposed to have taken place. Forested slopes lead out to Harbottle Hills to the south and west. Several rights-of-way climb them from the village, but take heed of the warning signs erected by the Ministry of Defence before following any of the moorland paths entering the Otterburn Artillery Ranges.

As with the rest of the villages along the eastern edge of the Northumberland National Park, **Holystone** is only a few hundred yards inside the boundary. This secluded hamlet above the west bank of the Coquet, is where St Paulinus is supposed to have baptized 3,000 Northumbrians during Easter week in 627. The site of this mammoth task was at Lady's Well, a rectangular pool fed by clear spring water and reached by a footpath from the Salmon Inn. There is a stone cross in the centre of the pool and a statue dedicated to St Paulinus at the side. Lady's Well is now owned by the National Trust.

Holystone Common, a forested outlier of the Cheviot Hills, is reached along a quiet, mile-long track to the south-west of the village. A group of tumuli on the common, known as the Five Barrows (NY954020) yielded evidence of a highly civilised population that lived in the area between 1600 and 1000BC. Many other prehistoric relics stand enigmatically on the windswept moorland heights, such as the line of stones known as the Five Kings and the earth ramparts of a fort above Harehaugh (NT970998).

A ruined peel tower stands in the grounds of Holystone Grange, a private house on the side road above the Coquet about $1^1/_2$ miles west of the tiny village of Hepple.

Moving downstream again along the Coquet, Thropton and its bigger neighbour Rothbury, 2 miles to the east, are just outside the park boundary, but very much linked to its everyday life. **Thropton** is divided almost equally by the Wreigh Burn, a tributary of the Coquet. An ancient humpbacked bridge crosses the burn and short footpaths can be used to explore both sides of the village. **Rothbury** has one of the most picturesque settings in Northumberland. The town is favoured by its sheltered position and is built on a series of natural terraces above the north bank of the River Coquet. Easy access to the Cheviot Hills and the Northumberland National Park has naturally led to the town's development as a holiday resort. Wooded hills to the north shelter Rothbury from all but the harshest winter storms. The town developed in the late thirteenth century, but it has roots reaching further into the past. Ancient cairns and settlements dot the surrounding heights and Christianity came early to the area. In the church a seventeenth-century font stands on a beautifully carved red sandstone cross shaft dating from around the beginning of the ninth century (the head is in the Museum of Antiquities, Newcastle upon Tyne). Below the church a medieval bridge, much altered by subsequent widening, still carries the B6342 over the Coquet on its triple arches.

New Town Park, below the Simonside Hills south of the town, was enclosed by Robert Rogerson in 1275 as a deerpark. Although occasional roe deer can be seen, little now remains of the wall surrounding this once extensive preserve, except for sections that appear along the roadside between Lordenshaw and Tosson. Across the Coquet an old peel tower stands in Gret Tosson, and another is at Whitton, directly above the valley bottom racecourse. Steeplechase meetings are held on the riverside racecourse, where there is also a golf course and a picnic site.

The area offers many short — or long — walks. Some, using the natural terraces on the northern hillside, wander between Rothbury and neighbouring Thropton. Across the valley Simonside Hill, 1,408ft (429m), is an easy 3-mile climb by way of a rough track that starts in Great Tosson and ascends through forest to craggy Raven's Heugh, 1,385ft (422m) to reach the summit of Simonside. Heugh means a hill which ends abruptly, (an escarpment). There is a National Park Information Centre in main street of Rothbury. Caravan sites at Whitton across the river have steep, but reasonable access.

Lord Armstrong's mansion at Cragside

 To the east, the Coquet flows through a narrow gap called the Thrum and above it rise wooded slopes surrounding **Cragside**, the mansion which Norman Shaw built between 1864 and 1884 for Sir William (later Lord) Armstrong. Combining elements of mock Tudor and Norman features, the house is very much in the 'Old English' revivalist style favoured by the Victorians; its heavy internal decor, massively ornate fireplaces and large doors are typical of an era that managed to combine prosperity and opulent living conditions for the successful together with low labour costs. Armstrong sur- rounded his retreat with landscaped gardens and forest. Graceful cast-iron bridges to his design cross the deep ravine, making ideal vantage points to admire Cragside's famed rhododendrons and azaleas. The 910 acres of woodland and nearby farms and forests, all part of the estate, are now owned by the National Trust.

Visitors to Cragside should allow themselves plenty of time to see not only the house, but also the meandering walks that follow gentle gradients throughout the gardens; or to follow the 'Power Circuit', a 3-mile circular walk that includes the restored Ram and Power Houses with their hydraulic and hydro-electric machinery, a visitor centre and Museum of Energy. Forest and lakeside drives together with a children's playground offer alternative relaxations.

Redesdale and the North Tyne

Moving west into Redesdale, the busy A68(T) Darlington to Edinburgh road follows the river to its source below **Carter Bar** on the border between England and Scotland. Carter Bar marks the highest point of the road, 1,370ft (418m) above sea level — a notorious place in winter, when it is frequently blocked by snow.

Following the A68 downstream along the Rede, the angle of descent eases alongside Catcleugh Reservoir and after another mile reaches **Byrness**, a Forestry Commission village built upstream of a tiny church dating from 1786 whose pretty churchyard fills with wild daffodils each spring. A 12-mile-long Forest Drive (toll road) from Kielder joins the A68 nearby, above the sturdy-looking farmhouse of Blakehopeburnhaugh. There is a forest nature trail above the farm. The Pennine Way crosses the A68 at Byrness where accommodation may be found.

Present-day soldiers using Redesdale Camp near **Rochester** are following the footsteps of Roman legionaries who camped at *Bremenium* fort, an important post on Dere Street north of Hadrian's ⊓ Wall. High Rochester Farm (NY834986) marks the site of the fort and although only a few mounds and parts of the west gateway and outer wall can be traced with any ease, there is a fine example of a bastle house from the time of the border raids. Artillery ranges and military practice areas beyond Redesdale Camp cover about 70sq miles of wild moorland stretching north-east towards the border and to Otterburn in the south. The road divides about 3 miles south-east of Rochester; the A696(T) starts at this point and runs on to Newcastle upon Tyne, while the A68(T) follows the National Park boundary to Corsenside Common and rushes through **West Woodburn**. This straggling village is just outside the park and is linked with its neighbour, East Woodburn, by a quiet lane following the south bank of the River Rede.

Habicantum Roman fort (NY891862) is nearby, to the east of a ⊓ bend in Dere Street. Most of the line of the Roman road is followed by the A68(T), but inexplicably it bypasses *Habicantum* in a wide dogleg to its east. The fort was one of the first outposts north-west along Dere Street from Hadrian's Wall, a days march from *Corstopitum*, near modern Corbridge. Regrettably little of the fort can be seen apart from the mound now standing on private land. A Roman milestone has been re-erected to the north of the village and marks the boundary of the Northumberland National Park.

A large 'pepperbox' cairn on Padon Hill (NY820928) north of an unclassified road from the A68 to the North Tyne valley, commemorates Alexander Padon, a Scottish Covenanter who held meetings on the site for religious dissenters in the seventeenth century. Traditionally the stones were carried one at a time by worshippers.

A quiet side road, the B6341, crosses a corner of the National Park to link the Rede and Coquet valleys. **Otterburn**, about a mile north-west of the junction of the 'B' road and the A696(T), straddles the main road. It makes an excellent centre for walking and fishing holidays in the area. Two seventeenth-century gentlemen's houses, Otterburn Hall and Otterburn Tower, offer accommodation together with coaching inns that earlier served traffic on the turnpike roads. There has been a mill by the side of the River Rede to the south of Otterburn for at least 700 years. The present mill, renowned for its fine quality tweeds and rugs, is about 150 years old.

The battle of Otterburn was fought nearby in 1388. Casualties from the battle are buried in St Cuthbert's churchyard in **Elsdon**. This compact village, built mainly to the west of Elsdon Burn, was once the capital of Redesdale. Today the village is mostly a cluster of eighteenth-century houses around the pleasant green. The four-teenth-century church has a half-barrel vaulted ceiling. The rectory is a fortified tower, one of the best preserved peel towers in Britain. Even older are the remains of a Norman motte and bailey. It stands beside the road on the Rothbury side of the village and was once topped by a palisaded wooden castle. An unclassified moorland road to the south-east of Elsdon crosses Battle Hill (NY950914) where there is a good view of Redesdale and after a mile reaches lonely Winter's Gibbet (NY963908). The site is marked by the replica of the gibbet where William Winter was hanged in 1791 for the murder of Margaret Crozier. The gruesome memorial is complete with a wooden effigy of Winter's head.

Further west, the River North Tyne rises as a series of tributary burns draining south-east within the outer limits of Kielder Forest. A minor road follows the valley and the first place of note is **Kielder**, a Forestry Commission village dating mostly from the 1950s, near the head of Kielder Reservoir. It was built to provide homes for workers in the nearby forests. The surrounding area was once open moorland and Kielder Castle was built in 1775 as a shooting lodge for the Duke of Northumberland; in recent times it became a palatial working men's club and presently houses an information centre. Kielder Castle Visitor Centre is open during the summer and houses an exhibition covering all aspects of timber growing and its uses; visiting groups can book the services of a ranger for guided walks. Northumbria Water also has a visitor centre at Tower Knowe. The Forest Drive, along a toll road, starts at Kielder Castle and threads its way through 12 miles of conifer plantations, with sections of open moorland, to join the A68 near Byrness.

A once important drove road crossed the border near Bloody Bush (NY571910), near the head of Akenshaw Burn about 4 miles south-west of Kielder. A stone pillar at this point acted as a waymark for cattle drovers and the name probably commemorates a border skirmish. It is still possible to follow the line of the drove road on foot, by a forest track above Akenshaw Burn continuing beyond the Forest Nature Trail. The 10-mile walk starts near the bridge across Lewis Burn (NY645904), about 3 miles south-east of Kielder.

Four linked forests together make **Kielder Forest**: Kielder, Falstone, Wark and Redesdale. Together they form Europe's largest man-made forest. A popular area for recreation, the forest offers peace and tranquillity and also space for competitive sports, ranging from orienteering to motor rallying. In winter, several forests drives are ideal for cross-country skiing. Brown trout inhabit many of the burns in Kielder, Falstone and Redesdale forests; rod licences are available from Northumbria Water, Yarrow Moor, Falstone, Hexham, and day or period permits from the District Forest Offices. Public access on foot is encouraged by waymarked walks and trails, as well as longer walks. Cars, however are restricted to the 12-mile Forest Drive (toll road) from Kielder village to Blakehopeburnhaugh on the A68 near Byrness. Camping and caravanning facilities are provided at Stonehaugh and Kielder, with other sites at Leaplish and Byrness. Holiday cabins have been established on sites throughout the forest. (For addresses, see Further Information.) Kielder Forest supports a large and varied wildlife population and observation hides are available for hire to individuals or groups.

It is fitting that Europe's largest man-made lake, Kielder Water, opened in 1982, should be surrounded by the largest man-made forest. The valley's contours have created a lake of a pleasing irregularity in shape, with bays and tiny, twisting estuaries. To prevent unsightly mudflats appearing in the shallower upper reaches during droughts, the smaller Bakethin dam was built to retain an auxiliary reservoir about 1 mile below Kielder Castle.

Picnic sites are strategically sited either on the shore or in the nearby forest. Car parking is easy and toilets for the disabled are available near most of them. Natural and man-made knolls make excellent viewpoints, and waymarked walks and trails connect several of the main features. Fishing and watersports of many kinds are available, and extensive field study facilities have been developed, both for school parties and visiting naturalists. The reservoir has settled into a naturalized state and wildlife, especially migrant waterfowl, has been attracted to Kielder. Special areas have been

Kielder Reservoir

kept free from outside pressures and the Bakethin portion of the reservoir has been made into a Nature Conservation Area.

Caravanning and campsites, which include facilities for backpacking together with attractive holiday cabins, are provided at several places around the reservoir. As well as water sports, cycle trails, orienteering courses, pony trekking, guided walks and in winter, cross-country skiing trails have been provided to complete the almost infinite number of activities possible on and around Kielder Water.

Below the dam, and unfortunately rather dominated by the holiday cabins associated with Kielder Water, the tiny village of **Falstone** was founded by Anglo-Saxon settlers. An eighth-century cross was found close by; inscriptions on it call for prayers for the souls of Hroethbert and Eoma. The cross is now in the keeping of the Newcastle Museum of Antiquities.

The minor road now follows the North Tyne gently down its partly wooded valley, past the welcoming doors of the Moorcock Inn. About a mile further on Chidron Burn, from the depths of Wark Forest, joins the North Tyne a hundred yards or so below Tarset Burn's confluence with the main river. This stream drains an area of moorland and forest to the north. The remote valley, served only by narrow winding lanes has several well-preserved examples of bastle-houses and towers. Of the latter, Tarset Castle (NY792856) in the valley bottom was once a farmhouse. Sixteenth-century Black Middens Bastle House (NY774900), near the boundary of Kielder Forest, is maintained by English Heritage.

Almost surrounded by, but not quite within the National Park, **Bellingham** (pronounced 'Bellinjam') was once the centre of a busy ironstone and coal mining area. This industry and the railway that served it have gone; today the town is an important market for sales of cattle and sheep bred on the nearby fells. St Cuthbert's body is supposed to have rested here during its long travels around the North before reaching Durham; the village church is therefore named after him. Historically, there has been a church on this site since the eleventh century; however, nothing remains from that time, the oldest features dating from the thirteenth, and most of the present building is early seventeenth century with nineteenth-century 'improvements'. Near the church is St Cuthbert's, or Cuddy's, Well whose waters were once claimed to have healing properties and are still used for baptisms.

A quiet town, Bellingham is the kind of place where you naturally look for bygones. The Boer War Memorial, together with a wooden Chinese gun captured at Fort Taku during the Boxer Rebellion, are just two of the unusual items to be found. The annual North Tyne Agricultural Show is held on riverside meadows below the town, usually on the last Saturday in August.

Reached by an attractive $1^1/_2$ mile footpath immediately beyond the old railway sidings north of Bellingham, the secluded wooded dell of **Hareshaw Linn** leads to a 30ft-high waterfall. Sturdy walkers pass through the town during the later (or earlier, if travelling south) stages of the Pennine Way, most seeking accommodation either in the town or at the nearby youth hostel. There is an information centre in the main street.

The south-western corner of the Northumberland National Park takes in Wark Forest, as well as the best preserved section of Hadrian's Wall and its attendant forts, using a section of Stanegate Roman road as its southern boundary. The Roman military area around Hadrian's Wall will be dealt with in a separate chapter, but before moving on, attention should be drawn to facilities in Wark Forest, which include campsites, forest walks and a deer farm, and also the attractions of Haughton Moor and its loughs. These include Comyn's Cross (NY799736), and dramatic views of Hadrian's Wall from the Pennine Way.

South-East of the National Park

This section deals with the rest of the east-flowing valleys south-east of the National Park as far as the A1(T). As a rough indication its boundaries may be taken as the A1 in the east, the A68 in the west, the Northumberland National Park in the north and B6318 as the southern boundary. Starting in the north at **Longframlington**, on the A697 about 9 miles north-west of Morpeth, where the village church dates from 1190. Built in Transitional style, its most interesting features are the Norman chancel arch with three detached pillars on either side of the nave and an ancient carved stone bench. The vestry has a delightfully carved Jacobean oak chest. There is a small display devoted to the history and manufacture of the Northumbrian smallpipe in the village. As it is run by volunteers, it is advisable to telephone in advance (see Further Information). Embleton Hall, a private residence on the main road to the north-west of the village church, is eighteenth century.

Devil's Causeway, the Roman road between Hadrian's Wall and the Scottish border, can be easily traced to the west of Longframlington. A farm lane south past Framlington Villa follows the route for about three-quarters of a mile.

A couple of miles south and well hidden from any other habitation, **Brinkburn Priory** fits into a tight wooded bend of the River Coquet. The approach is along a side lane off the B6334, Rothbury road, about $1^1/_2$ miles west of its junction with the A697. The priory was founded by William de Bertram, first Baron Mitford in about 1135. After the Dissolution of the Monasteries in the sixteenth century it became a private house, but later fell into disuse and was a complete ruin by 1858; its roof was missing and part of the nave had collapsed. Brinkburn was carefully restored by Thomas Austin, a Newcastle architect, and the building now stands as an almost perfect example of early Gothic architecture. It is now in the care of English Heritage and is open to the public from mid-March to mid-October.

Turning now to the valley of the Wansbeck and its tributaries; the most northerly is the River Font which starts its life by draining the moorland surrounding Harwood Forest. A group of side burns join to form Fontburn Reservoir and from it flows the Font itself to meander gently south-east through woodlands and steadily improving farmlands towards its confluence with the River Wansbeck. **Netherwitton** is built above a wide stretch of the Font. The present manor house, Netherwitton Hall, is early eighteenth century, but there has been a dwelling on the site since the fourteenth century. The remains of a Georgian mill are on the riverbank close to the road bridge, where there is also a good view of the hall. Two miles further to the north-west, at the end of a wooded side lane, is where John Dobson built Nunnykirk Hall, one of his finest works.

Downstream again, **Mitford** fills the space immediately west of the wooded junction of the Font and Wansbeck, and is separated from Morpeth by the A1 which crosses the Wansbeck along a viaduct. Two stately and venerable bridges lead in and out of this unspoilt village, that to the south leading to Mitford Castle whose ruined five-sided keep, destroyed by the Scots around 1318, dominates the skyline above the steep riverbank. A Norman church stands separate from the main village; Mitford was moved to its present position after the original village was sacked by King John in 1216. Most of the church of St Mary Magdalene was reconstructed in 1875, but several eleventh-century features are still recognisable, including a fine example of a priest's doorway and its typically Norman chevron moulding. A most attractive triple window lights the east end of the church.

A loop of the Wansbeck almost surrounds Mitford Hall. Another of John Dobson's designs, it dates from 1828 and replaced an older and less convenient building closer to the village. Little remains of the latter apart from a battlemented tower dated 1673.

Hart Burn, the next tributary of the Wansbeck, joins the latter about 4 miles west of the Font. Its namesake village, **Hartburn**, is a sheltered hamlet at the top of a steep hill that leads down to the river. There is a delightfully unspoiled, mainly thirteenth-century church here that is associated with the Knight's Templars. Dogtooth moulding decorates both sides of the south doorway, and in the nave the cup-shaped font is supported by a central pillar and three side-shafts. There are several interesting tomb brasses and a memorial to John Hodgson, a local historian who wrote extensively about Northumberland and also traced the line of the Devil's Causeway Roman road, which passes a little over a quarter of a mile to the north-west of Hartburn.

Downstream, and on the north bank above the junction with the Wansbeck, **Meldon Park** is the focal point of a scattered rural community in lush farmland to the south of the B6343, about 5 miles west of Morpeth. John Dobson built Meldon Park for himself in 1831. The grounds of the house are usually open to the public on advertised days in summer, as part of the Northumbria Garden Scheme. July is the best month, when the rose garden and herbaceous borders are at their most colourful. Meldon church is about a mile to the south; although its foundations date from the thirteenth century, the present building is mainly Victorian.

Moving now into the Wansbeck valley, the first place of note is **Kirkwhelpington**. The A696 passes the village to the west, leaving behind a cluster of stone houses above the infant river. John Hodgson, the historian, lived here between 1823 and 1832. St Bartholomew's Church was founded in Norman times, but the building is mostly thirteenth century with later additions, especially during the prosperous Victorian era; the tower is built in the Perpendicular style. Sir Charles Parsons, the inventor of the steam turbine, lived nearby and was buried in the churchyard in 1931.

Ordnance Survey maps refer to the nearby moorland as Kirkwhelpington Common, but locals know it as the Wilds of Wannie, after the name of the local river, the Wansbeck.

Kirkharle Estate is a mile or so to the south-east, on both sides of the A696. The hall is Victorian, but the tiny estate chapel dedicated to St Wilfrid is a fourteenth-century building on Norman foundations. 'Capability' Brown, the landscape artist and garden designer, was born near by in 1715 and as a boy developed the foundations of his craft by working in the estate gardens.

The heads of four mythical beasts greet the visitor to **Wallington Hall**. Surrounded by woodland above the north bank of the Wansbeck, the stately home and parkland together with an estate covering 12,970 acres is now owned by the National Trust. The house was built in 1688, but greatly altered in the 1740s. Its interior has fine rococo plasterwork by Italian craftsmen and there is porcelain, needlework, furniture and a collection of doll's houses displayed in rooms ranging from an early Georgian saloon to a late Victorian nursery and kitchen. The central hall dates from the mid-nineteenth century, and was designed by John Dobson who decorated it with wall paintings by William Bell Scott. Outside is a walled garden, with a conservatory specializing in fuchsias, a coach museum, Chinese pond, lakes and woodlands. 'Capability' Brown began his professional career here. The grounds are open all the year and the house and gardens on advertised days.

About 1^1/$_2$ miles to the south of the River Wansbeck, **Bolam Lake Country Park** is an artificial lake in a woodland setting about 2 miles north-west of Belsay. Access is along country lanes linking the A696 and B6343; there are picnic sites and car parking facilities. The lake and nearby estate of Bolam Hall were created by John Dobson in the nineteenth century. The hall, a mile to the north-east of the lake, is now a guesthouse; the hall and St Andrew's Church are the only remaining links with an older village. The church dates from 960 and is one of the best-preserved Saxon churches in Northumberland. Its tower is the oldest feature, but much of the Saxon work can still be

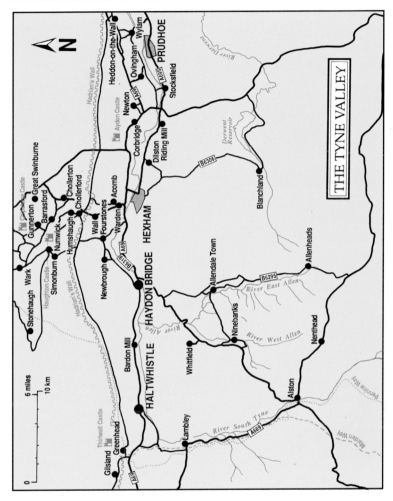

found within the Norman interior.

Shortflatt Tower to the south of the lake is a private house, built on the remains of a fourteenth-century peel tower. **Shaftoe Crags** (NZ054823), a prominent outcrop topped by a prehistoric fort to the west of Bolam Houses, can be approached along a mile-long public footpath beyond the crossroads. Nearby is a standing stone with the strange name of Poind and his Man. The B6524 Morpeth to Belsay road makes a dog-leg through **Whalton**, an agricultural village of light-brown houses beside wide grassy verges. A number of the houses, including the rectory, are built around peel towers. The manor house was originally four cottages which were converted into a single dwelling by Sir Edwin Lutyens in 1908. Its gardens were designed by Gertrude Jekyll. The village is designated as a conservation area. The village church of St Mary is unusually wide for its length. Norman in origin, most of the building dates from the thirteenth century and was restored in 1908. Whalton is one of the few places to light a bael fire on Midsummer's Eve. The massive bonfire is probably a link with the pagan beliefs of the Viking settlers in the area. The rural hamlet of **Ogle** lies 2 miles to the south of Whalton and about the same distance from the A696 and Belsay, which are to its west; Ogle Castle is a Victorian restoration of a fifteenth- to sixteenth-century tower house.

Lush farmland fills the final corner made by the A68 and B6318 north of the Tyne valley. The A696 runs through **Belsay**. A ruined castle and Belsay Hall stand in parkland at the end of a mile of tree-lined drive. The site has been populated for thousands of years, with each successive development moving east across the centuries. The first was a circular mound to the west, built in prehistoric times by Neolithic people, and a standing stone associated with it later became a Christian cross. In the fourteenth century a castle was built to protect the tenants and a village clustered around its defensive walls. All that remains of the castle is an impressively ruined tower house and its adjacent wings. The last stage of the development came in the early nineteenth century when the village was demolished to make way for Belsay Hall, home of Sir Charles Monck, a member of the Middleton family. Designed by John Dobson, its south front is adorned by Doric pilasters and the spacious central hall surrounded by Ionic and Doric columns in the romantic style of the time. The grounds are particularly fine, with a lake and a quarry garden. Hall, castle and gardens are open to the public from mid-March to mid-October, together with an exhibition of the development of the estate. The demolished village was replaced in 1830 by the single arcade of Italianate sandstone buildings seen on the A696. There is a particularly impressive view of Belsay Castle from the Belsay-Stamfordham road (B6309). **Stamfordham** is an elongated village of Georgian terraced houses built around an exceptionally long green above the River Pont. There is a preaching cross dated 1736 and a gaol house. The thirteenth-century church stands at the western side of the village with its part Tudor, part eighteenth-century vicarage on the opposite side of the river. The village is a conservation area and is rightly proud of the number of times it has won the annual award for the Best Kept Village in Northumberland. A fair is held on the village green every Whit Monday.

THE TYNE VALLEY

The Tyne, the North-East's major river, carves its way due east to the industrial coast. Fed by north and south flowing tributaries, it is unpolluted for most of its length and in its upper reaches is a good sporting river for anglers. All the main side rivers rise from high moorland springs; only the North Tyne rises in the north, but from the south, the South Tyne, West and East Allens, Devil's Water and the Derwent increase its size as the Tyne flows steadily eastward. Most of the important towns line the main valley and high remote villages, one time centres of lead mining are tucked away in sheltered spots among the western dales. Industrial towns, many of them now radically changed, are to the south-west of Newcastle upon Tyne, the focal point of industry and commerce for Tyneside.

The South-Tyne, the most westerly tributary, rises on Cross Fell, 2,930ft (893m), the highest point in the Pennines and strictly in Cumbria, as is **Alston**, England's highest market town; the covered market stance fronts a group of four-storied old buildings lining a sharp bend of the steep cobbled main street. The market was created in 1154 for the benefit of the 'King's Miners'. Lead was the reason for Alston's development and it became the centre of an extensive mining field until the mid-1800s when lead prices fell dramatically.

For a short distance below Alston, the Pennine Way follows the Maiden Way, a Roman road south from Hadrian's Wall. The modern route skirts the complex ramparts of Whitley Castle, a Roman 'police post' whose correct name is not known. At Lambley, a one-time colliery hamlet, the Pennines can be said to end; beyond it the Tyne Gap and the beginning of the border fells. The large castellated private dwelling of Featherstone Castle on an unclassified side road lower down the valley, is built in the romantic style, but based on the site of an 800-year-old fortification guarding a river crossing.

Nenthead, an 'outlier' of the Alston mining complex, is at the top of its namesake valley. Many of the buildings associated with processing lead ore and also mining equipment have been restored and are now part of a mining trail around Nenthead village. A mile or two down the valley, the smaller Nentsberry Mining and Farming Museum, a collection of old mining equipment and farming implements, is based on a pub and children's play area.

Eastwards across the moors are the twin dales of the West and East Allen, both now much quieter than in their heyday of lead mining. Tiny hamlets line West Allendale and at Ninebanks, a miners' barracks, or 'shop' where they lived during the week, there is now an attractive little youth hostel used by walkers and cyclists exploring this quiet valley. **Whitfield**, the main village in this dale, nestles in a secluded woodland setting on a side road off the A686, about 6 miles south-west of Haydon Bridge. Whitfield Hall is mid-eighteenth century, but is probably built on the site of an older house. The village church dates from 1860 and stands at the side of the main road close to the hall's northern boundary. There is a riverside caravan site a mile to the south at Low Harber.

The East Allen rises below the boundary with County Durham, high on Wolfcleugh Common and the B6295 from Weardale drops steeply through Allenheads Park to **Allendale**, a former mining community, now the estate village of the nearby hall and park. With the declining fortunes of the valley and a much smaller population, several redundant schools and chapels now serve as field study centres for the area. Pony trekking takes place from Allenheads in summer and the surrounding moors are suitable for skiing in winter.

The main centre for both valleys is **Allendale Town**. Another former lead-mining town, it has the rolling heatherclad moors of Hexhamshire Common and the northern Pennines as a backcloth. A sundial in the market place declares the town to be the geographical centre of Britain.

Move now into the main valley. The river is still the South Tyne, but its character is well established by the time it reaches Haltwhistle, a character which continues eastwards, joined by the North Tyne above Hexham, all the way to the sea. The most westerly habitation in Northumberland is **Gilsland**, a small village on the western side of the Tyne-Solway gap, 2 miles north-west of Greenhead along the B6318 Langholme Road. Hadrian's Wall passes through the village and a section of it is visible in the vicarage garden. (For further details, see Chapter 3). Gilsland has romantic links with the novelist Sir Walter Scott. It was here that he met his future wife, Charlotte Carpenter, and part of *Guy Mannering* is set in the village.

Greenhead sits in a tight green hollow at the junction of the B6318 and A69(T). The river is Tipalt Burn and the site of the village is on a natural river crossing which has been in use from before Roman times. Both the Maiden Way and Stanegate Roman roads crossed at this point, serving Hadrian's Wall (see Chapter 3). Stones from the Wall were removed by General Wade in the eighteenth century to build a military road which later became the B6318. Now bypassed by the busy A69, Greenhead makes an ideal starting point to explore the middle part of Hadrian's Wall. John Dobson of Newcastle designed the present nineteenth-century church, though a church

has stood on the site since Saxon times. Fourteenth-century Thirlwall
Castle, a little to the north of Greenhead stands beside Tipalt Burn.
Now a romantic ruin still guarding a natural gap in the east-west
escarpment, it was used as base by Edward I, Hammer of the Scots,
for one of his forays into Scotland in 1306.

The A69 descends towards the Tyne, passing Blenkinsopp Castle, a group of buildings that are part sixteenth-century ruin, part
private seventeenth-century manor house. About a mile further east
is Blenkinsopp Hall, a privately owned nineteenth-century house of
some distinction standing in attractive gardens that are open on
advertised days during the summer.

Haltwhistle is built above a broad sweep of the South Tyne, a
busy little industrial and market town, supplying the needs of
nearby villages and farms on the remote surrounding fells. The town
is a useful centre for visiting the north Pennines, Hadrian's Wall, or
the upper reaches of the South Tyne valley. Notable buildings in and
around the town centre range from the Old Court House in Central
Place to the Red Lion. The latter incorporates a peel tower, a relic of
the turbulent past of this district, where townspeople and their
animals would shelter when threatened by marauding Scots. Holy
Cross, the parish church, is thirteenth century and claims to have
been founded by William, Lyon King of Scotland in 1178. (At one
time the border was far to the south of its present position and most
of Northumbria and Cumbria were part of Scotland). The plain
exterior gives little indication of the spacious interior; its pride is the
painted roof of the nave, a Victorian embellishment. A nature trail
starts on the outskirts of the town and visits several nearby Roman
sites (see Chapter 3 for further details). The South Tyne Show is held
on a riverside meadow close to the town.

Bellister Castle is across the Tyne, half a mile south of
Haltwhistle. Owned by the National Trust, the Victorian castle is on
the site of an older building of which a peel tower, incorporated into
the house, still remains. Apart from rights of way the estate, of castle,
three farms, and cottages, is not open to the public.

Several minor roads link the A69 with Hadrian's Wall to its north;
Bardon Mill, about half way between Haltwhistle and Hexham, is
served by one of them. The former colliery village surrounds the
mouth of deep-cut Brackies Burn before it joins the South Tyne. A
tourist bus runs from the Tyne valley, on a circular route calling at
most of the important features along the central section of Hadrian's
Wall, including *Vindolanda* and Housesteads.

Across the river from Bardon Mill, the small village of
Beltingham near the mouth of the River Allen, is only accessible by

a narrow side road off the A69. The church, although much altered in the nineteenth century, was probably founded in the early part of the sixteenth century as a chapel of ease. Dedicated to St Cuthbert, it is reputed to have Saxon origins; certainly the age of a yew tree in the churchyard seems to bear that out. Two Roman altarstones, also in the churchyard, link the building to even older times. An elegant Georgian house next to the church belongs to the Bowes-Lyon family, relatives of the Queen Mother.

Eighteenth-century Ridley Hall is over the fields from Beltingham and close to the River Allen. The mock castle is now a college and holiday centre. A mile south of the hall and best reached by 2 miles of footpaths are the National Trust property of Allen Banks and the beauty spot of Plankey Mill. Another mile-long path leads from the mill to Staward Pele (NY799608). Quiet lanes and field paths lead back to Ridley Hall, although the outer woodland path in reverse is probably the more attractive way.

On down the valley to **Haydon Bridge**, a village which developed around a crossing of the South Tyne. Its church is built on hallowed ground where St Cuthbert's body rested during its long journey around Northumbria. A former spa, the village is a cluster of snug grey stone houses filling the level ground on both sides of the river. The grammar school was founded by the Shafto Trust in 1685. The song *Bobby Shafto's Gone to Sea* was written about one of the family as an election ditty. The A69 crosses the river here by a utilitarian reinforced concrete bridge, which leaves the old six-arched stone bridge to pedestrians. Frequent heavy flooding by the South Tyne damaged this eighteenth-century bridge and the structure was deemed unsafe, as well as awkward for heavy traffic. The A69 is joined by the A686 (Alston road), a little under half a mile to the east of Haydon Bridge. Two miles further is Langley Castle, a massive Victorian reconstruction of a fourteenth-century oblong fortification with four guardian corner towers. At one time or other it was owned by most of the great Northumbrian families, but is now a restaurant specialising in medieval banquets.

Before moving on to the River Tyne itself, a short diversion into the valley of the North Tyne is necessary, to complete the description as far as the southern boundary of the Northumberland National Park. (For the rest of the North Tyne northwards, see the National Park section of this chapter). A quiet side road from Warden follows the west bank of the river as far as Chollerford. From there the B6320 can be used to reach the National Park boundary before returning downstream and above the east bank of the North Tyne to its confluence with the main river.

Warden, a secluded hamlet on a side road linking the A69 and B6319, is built above the flood plain of a river which can still rise with alarming rapidity. The wooded slopes of High Warden Hill rise above the village, and its sandstone summit, 587ft above sea level, is crowned by an extensive Iron Age fort. A $5^1/_2$ mile walk through High Warden village passes the fort and returns by way of Fourstones and the riverside. Warden's church is Saxon and Norman, dating from 1050, but incorporates many Roman stones taken from the nearby Hadrian's Wall. Boat Inn is beside the bridge across the South Tyne and to the west is one of the oldest papermills in England — it dates from 1763.

The North Tyne is considered to be the most attractive of all the tributaries; its gentle wood-lined meanders offer sport for the angler and side turnings off the valley road, the B6320, lead down to charming views. The Romans built a cavalry fort, *Cilurnum* (see Chapter 3), on the west side of the river which was crossed by a defended bridge. The B6318 Heddon-on-the-Wall to Greenhead road, the Military Way, crosses the river upstream of the Roman bridge at **Chollerford**, a small group of buildings and an inn built around the northern abutment of the single-track bridge. A traffic island opposite the George Hotel marks the junction of the B6318 and B6320 Bellingham road. The bridge dates from 1778 and replaced an earlier one washed away in 1771. The George, a former coaching house, is a favourite venue for anglers. A minor road leaves the B6320 at the Chollerford island and makes a wide loop above the river, before rejoining the B road a couple of miles further along the valley.

Humshaugh sits on rising ground above the river, a tiny village built around a comfortable looking red-brick Georgian manor house. Although built on ancient foundations, the present church dates from 1818, to a design by John Dobson of Newcastle. Haughton Castle, a riverside stronghold north of the village, dates from before the fourteenth century, but frequent sackings and burnings led to its abandonment in the sixteenth century. The present building is a nineteenth-century restoration together with additional features by Anthony Salvin who was responsible for many fine Northumbrian mansions. Both Humshaugh House and Haughton Castle are privately owned, but the gardens are occasionally open on advertised days.

White painted cottages clustered around a village green in **Simonburn** belong to estate workers from nearby Nunwick House. The village proper is on a side road to the west of the B6320, where St Mungo's, the village church, is the eighteenth- and nineteenth-century version of a church which has stood on the site since the thirteenth century. Despite its rebuilding, the floor slopes towards the altar, giving the impression of great age.

Nunwick House, a private dwelling to the east of the valley road, is built of red sandstone and dates from 1740, reputedly designed by William Adam, but with later additions by Bonomi. The garden is famous for its alpines and herbaceous borders, as well as semi-formal woodlands, and is open to the public on advertised dates.

Simonburn Castle is about three quarters of a mile west of the village in the middle of a wood. The ruins of the fourteenth-century tower house can be reached by a public right-of-way which starts at Burn House, north-west of Simonburn. A side road opposite the entrance to Nunwick House, about a quarter of a mile beyond the village, leads towards Wark Forest (see Stonehaugh). The road passes Ravensheugh Crags along the way and also the Goatstones, a stone circle. One of the four stones bears cup markings which date from about 1,600 to 1,000BC.

The tree-lined B6320 continues upstream along the North Tyne through lush pastureland. The major feature you will see on entering the pleasant village of **Wark**, is a steep grassy bank, all that remains of a Norman motte and bailey castle. The village, a pleasant grouping of attractive houses set back from delightful cottage gardens, spreads from a crossroads surrounded by a wide village green. A sixteenth-century farmhouse to one side of the green is now the curiously named Battlesteads Inn. Quiet roads to the west lead into Wark Forest and the amenities around the Forestry Commission village of Stonehaugh.

The B6320 crosses the North Tyne and enters Bellingham (see National Park section of this chapter). Winding by-roads connect small villages lying between the A68 and the east bank of the river. A side road past Bellingham's school crosses level riverside pasture and over the Rede into Redesmouth village. From there a complex of even narrower lanes lead through Birtley to a junction with a road from Wark to Chollerton on the A6079. **Chipchase Castle** is about a mile downstream along this road. The castle, considered to be one of the finest examples of Jacobean architecture in Northumberland, stands at the head of parkland rising above the east bank of the North Tyne. It was built in 1621 around a fourteenth-century peel tower for the Heron family, official 'keepers' of Tynedale. The castle and its eighteenth-century chapel are in private grounds, but can be seen from the B6320 across the river. The name Chipchase may derive from Old English words meaning 'beam' or 'log'.

Moving away from the river for the moment, **Gunnerton**, an agricultural village, is built at the foot of its wooded dene. St

Christopher's Church was built in 1900 to the prize-winning design of a young architect named Hall, who later took holy orders and became a hermit. A motte and bailey defensive mound can be found in private woodland half a mile to the north.

The side road leads north-east to **Pity Me**, a woodland hamlet not far from the A68. There is a camping and caravan site in Barrasford Park. 'Pity Me' may indicate the site of a former pond or lake (*petit mere*), as in the case of its Durham namesake. Ignoring the main road, the side road loops round to **Great Swinburne**, another woodland hamlet, this time above the Swin Burn (without the 'e'), which flows through a wooded ravine below the village. Most of the houses are occupied by workers from the estate of seventeenth-century Swinburne Castle, which is privately owned. Half a mile to the south and in a private field above Coal Burn (NY937745), is the largest standing stone in the county. This red sandstone monolith is 12ft high and 3ft wide, with incised grooves running down its sides and is decorated with enigmatic 'cup and ring' markings.

Regain the river at **Barrasford**, where a ferry once carried passengers across the North Tyne to Haughton Castle, a service which regrettably no longer operates. Walkers can still enjoy the view however, by following three quarters of a mile of riverside footpath downstream, then crossing the abandoned railway line to follow the road back for about the same distance to Barrasford.

The minor road joins the A6079 above the east bank of the river at **Chollerton**, near to where the battle of Heavenfield is reputed to have been fought in 634. The battlefield is marked by a simple roadside cross beside the B6318 (NY937696); St Oswald's chapel is in the middle of the field behind the cross. Chollerton's church is Norman, incorporating Roman pillars to support its south arcade. A Roman altar stands immediately inside the church door.

The A6079 continues downstream beyond its hazardous crossing of the B6318. After a mile the main road passes through **Wall**. The oldest part of the village is hidden from the road by later development, but the original village is a glorious cluster of tiny greens and charming dwellings, an ideal centre for exploring Hadrian's Wall. The originator of this timeless tourist attraction is commemorated in the name of the local inn.

Acomb is built mostly along a side road to the east of the A6079, above the confluence of the North and South Tyne rivers. The village is in two parts, old and new, the latter being closest to the main road. Acomb was once a coal mining community, but is now favoured by Tyneside commuters. The original village is composed mostly of eighteenth-century houses, built around a pleasant square marked by a Victorian drinking fountain. The manor house dates from 1736 and the opulently decorated church, a little to the south of Acomb, was designed by John Dobson, built in 1875, and enlarged 10 years later. There is a woodland caravan and camp site on reclaimed colliery land to the north-east of the village.

Now happily bypassed by the A69 trunk road and sited well above any danger of flooding by the Tyne, **Hexham**, the administrative centre of Tynedale is 1,300 years old, a market town living comfortably hand-in-hand with modern industry. The town developed around a crossing of the Tyne, where for centuries passengers were ferried over the river. The first bridge was not built until 1770 and was washed away by floods a year later. The next, erected in 1780, survived only two years before suffering a similar fate. However, the third dates from 1793 and still stands, although it had to be widened in 1967 to cope with the needs of modern traffic.

St Wilfrid built his abbey in Hexham in 674; an early use of stone by the Anglo-Saxons. The abbey suffered many attacks but gradually developed into the majestic focal point it is today; its initially dark medieval interior gives a cosy welcome to each visitor. The oldest remains of the original abbey can be found in the Saxon crypt; and St Wilfrid's chair, once used as a frith or sanctuary stool, is at least 1,300 years old and is reputed to be the coronation seat of the kings of Northumbria. The abbey has a Breeches Bible dating from 1612 amongst its collection of venerable books. Only the priory gate and chapter house remain from the once extensive buildings that supported this abbey. Their demise dates from the Dissolution of the Monasteries by Henry VIII.

The market place is in front of the abbey. The site is centuries old, continuing a tradition dating back beyond the Middle Ages. Beyond it is the gate-like Moot Hall, built in 1335 using convenient Roman materials. Its walls are 11ft thick, and it was once used as a debtor's prison. Round the corner is the Manor Office, also fourteenth century, a fortified tower again made from Roman stones. The building now houses the Middle March Centre, a museum of border history. Narrow streets lined with Georgian buildings wind away from the market place. The town holds busy agricultural markets, selling thousands of sheep and cattle each year. On a broad sweep to the south-west of the town, Hexham racecourse hosts National Hunt races. The course is used as a caravan and camping site between race meets.

East along the valley road for a little way, is **Dilston**, a tiny hamlet between Hexham and Corbridge. The name means 'homestead on Devil's Water', the wooded stream flowing north through the village to join the Tyne. Devil's Water itself is thought to be an Anglicisation of a Celtic name meaning 'black water'. Nearby are the ruins of an incomplete castle that was being built for the third Earl of Derwentwater at the time of his execution. A more recent building is Dilston Hall, now an advanced social training unit run by the county council, but once the home of Viscount Allendale.

Narrow winding lanes leading up to the valley head and no further make easy access to the small villages on either side of Devil's Water. Several short footpaths can be used to explore the middle section of this attractive valley, which is steeped in romantic history.

From Dilston, the B6307 climbs beside Dipton Wood to join the B6306 which is followed through Slaley Forest to **Blanchland** on the county boundary. There is a timeless serenity about this small moorland village in the wooded upper reaches of the Derwent Valley. Mellow grey stone houses fit snuggly around an open square opposite the Georgian comfort of the Lord Crewe Arms, and a narrow hump-backed bridge completes the tranquil rural scene. The present layout of the village dates from the early part of the eighteenth century, when the trustees of the Crewe estate built the cottages to house lead miners.

The name Blanchland links the place with its ecclesiastical foundations. White canons of the Augustinian order of Premonstratensians founded the abbey here in the twelfth century. After the Dissolution, the monks were driven away, but the abbey church was spared and remained in use by the local community. Renovated in the nineteenth century, little remains of the original fabric, apart from the tower and north transept.

Back again to the Tyne and over the bridge into **Corbridge**, once the capital of Anglo-Saxon Northumbria and now a delightful jumble of styles with many of its older houses built from Roman stones taken from nearby *Corstopitum* (for further details see Chapter 3). A civilian town that later became Corbridge developed around the fort from the third century AD. Time has left a wealth of historic buildings, not only at Roman *Corstopitum*, but in the town itself. Vicars of Corbridge built themselves a peel tower out of Roman stones, as protection against Scottish raids. The tower, which stands in a corner of the churchyard, now finds a more peaceful use as an information centre. The church is dedicated to St Andrew and is Saxon, with parts dating from before 786, but with later additions mainly from the thirteenth century onwards. A Roman gateway taken intact from *Corstopitum* supports the tower. The cast-iron market cross in the town square bears the Percy lion and dates from 1814. A seven-arched bridge below the town dates from 1674, the

Hexham market place and Moot Hall

only one to survive a disasterous flood in 1771; a less attractive Bailey bridge next to it protects the old structure from the excessive weight of modern traffic. A little further upstream, and visible during periods of drought, are the remains of piers of the original Roman bridge which carried Dere Street into *Corstopitum*.

Jacobean plotters are said to have held secret meetings in the Angel Hotel in Main Street. The present building is eighteenth century, but built on earlier foundations. Old shops and the Heron House Art Gallery complete the attractions of this interesting and historic town. A half-mile riverside footpath connects Corbridge with *Corstopitum*.

At the end of a minor road 2 miles to the north of Corbridge is the secluded hamlet of **Halton**, guarded by two ancient castles and with Hadrian's Wall to the north. Halton Tower is a Jacobean manor house added onto a fourteenth-century peel tower. Although the house is privately owned, the gardens usually take part in the Northumbrian Gardens Scheme each July. The village chapel is seventeenth century, built on eighth-century foundations. Wooded denes and lanes lead to Aydon Castle, and a mile to the south is a fortified manor house of similar age which has been restored by English Heritage.

The Hunday National Tractor Museum is at **Stocksfield**, on the A695. The museum is a collection of vintage tractors and farm machinery; many exhibits are in working order, together with scenes of farm life and shops from bygone times. A narrow-gauge railway completes the attractions. The Thomas Bewick Birthplace Museum is close by at Cherryburn. The cottage of this famous eighteenth-century wildlife engraver has been made into an introductory exhibition, displaying many of his original printing blocks and examining his life and work.

Bywell is just across the river, where village, castle, hall and two churches cluster around a south-facing promontory above a bend in the Tyne. The castle is a fifteenth-century tower with four turrets built mostly from Roman stones; it is privately owned and not open to the public. Bywell Hall, one of the seats of the Fenwick family, is a 1760 conversion of an older house with nineteenth-century alterations and beautifully landscaped gardens. Again this is a private house, but the gardens and riverside walk are open on advertised days. Because of a quirk in the parish boundaries, the village has two churches known locally as Black and White. St Andrew's was founded by the White Canons of Blanchland and is Saxon (the tower is particularly good) with thirteenth-century and later additions. St Peter's was founded in Norman times by Black Dominican Friars.

Industry and residential conurbations increase the closer one gets to Newcastle, but links with the past and interesting by-ways can be found around every corner. **Ovingham** has stood on the north bank of the Tyne since Saxon times. A packhorse way once came through the village, crossing Whittle Burn, a tributary of the Tyne, by a small bridge that still stands near the Bywell road. The parish church of St Mary was founded by Augustinian canons; the tower is part Saxon and although the interior is mostly thirteenth century, the rest of the building is the result of seventeenth- and nineteenth-century restoration. The vicarage to its south is early seventeenth-century. Ovingham holds an annual Goose Fair on the third Saturday in June, together with other traditional Northumbrian events. There is a caravan site on the edge of Horsley Wood about three quarters of a mile north-east of the village.

A minor road crosses the Tyne to reach the former colliery town of **Prudhoe** on the A695. Now a dormitory town with a large industrial estate, the town is old despite its appearance, and once had a castle to guard an important crossing over the Tyne. Buillt in 1173 during the reign of Henry II, the best remaining features are the gatehouse and a fourteenth-century barbican. The castle is now cared for by English Heritage; there is an exhibition of the history of the castle and a video presentation on Northumberland castles in the nineteenth-century 'gothic' house in the inner ward.

Two villages occupying the narrow strip between the Tyne and the A69(T) complete this chapter; **Wylam** on the north bank of the river can claim to be the birthplace of the railway age, for it was here in 1813 that William Hedley built his *Puffing Billy* to haul wagon loads of coal from Wylam Colliery to Lemington Staithes, a simple quay, about 4 miles down the Tyne. George Stephenson is usually the better known of the two pioneers. He was born at Wylam, in a cottage which still stands to the east of the village. Although owned by the National Trust, the cottage is not open to the public. The railway no longer runs through Wylam. The old track is followed by the Wylam and Wallbottle Wagonway through the Tyne Riverside Country Park. The 9-mile path passes Stephenson's Cottage and returns along the riverbank.

Two miles to the north-east and close by the county boundary of Northumberland and Tyne and Wear, is **Heddon-on-the-Wall**. Originally an agricultural village it developed into a residential suburb of Newcastle upon Tyne after World War II. The old village was built on ancient foundations and the hilltop church of St Andrew dates from Anglo-Saxon and Norman times. A terrace of miners' cottages built in 1796, was allocated to French Royalist refugees, an act of charity commemorated in the name Frenchmen's Row.

The most easterly visible section of Hadrian's Wall is to the east of Heddon and can be approached either from the B6318, or from the Heddon exit off the A69(T). A hoard of 5,000 silver coins, dating from 244-75 was found beneath a nearby milecastle in 1879.

Selected Walks

Hareshaw Linn
4 miles • Easy woodland stroll • 2 hours • Muddy after rain
Map OS 1:50000 Landranger Series Sheet 80.

This easy to follow walk starts in Bellingham on the B6320 in the upper North Tyne valley. Take the West Woodburn road as far as the river and cross the bridge. Turn left and follow the riverside lane, under the old railway bridge and as far as a row of cottages. Keep to the left of the cottages and follow the path directly ahead into the wooded ravine of Hareshaw Burn. The path keeps to the east side of the stream for about 1$^1/_4$ miles, then using plank bridges switches from side to side as far as the linn (waterfall). There is no right of way beyond this point, so return by the outward route and admire the views from another aspect.

Dustanburgh Castle

4$^1/_2$ miles • Easy coastal walk • 2 hours
Map OS 1:50000 Landranger Series Sheets 75 and 81.

The ancient pile of Dunstanburgh Castle dominates the wild rocky headland beyond the tiny fishing village of Craster (signposted from the B1339, north-east of Alnwick). From the car park walk towards Craster village and bear left around the harbour. Go through a gate and follow the coastal path as far as the castle. After visiting the castle, leave by the main gate and turn right along the footpath through the golf course as far as Dunstan Steads Farm. Go through the farmyard and turn left along the lane to Dunstan Square, where a left turn joins a field path towards a line of crags known as The Heughs. Turn right beneath the crags and follow the path back to the car park.

The walk may be extended by following the Arnold Memorial Trail from the car park, a short, but interesting geological trail.

Between Two Tynes

4 miles • Moderate-one climb • 2 hours
Map OS 1:50000 Landranger Series Sheet 87.

Here is a pleasant walk over a hill where our earliest forebears once lived, then down to a village with a pub, where a riverside stroll along the South Tyne leads back to its junction with the South Tyne. The walk starts at Bridge End, near an ancient road bridge and signposted from the A69 near Hexham. From the Boat Inn walk along the Warden road for about 60yd (55m) and turn left along a footpath signposted to Quality Cottages, then turn right. Follow a track uphill through a small wood. Cross a series of fields, keeping close to a hedge, and aim for a second wood. At the wood turn left and follow an obvious track past two further sections of woodland, to a cottage. Turn left at the cottage and walk downhill, changing sides along the wall as indicated by the track. Cross farmland to enter Fourstones village (pub). Walk through the village and turn left at the crossroads, then go down the lane, over a level crossing and continue as far as the riverbank. Turn left and follow the river downstream. After about a mile (1.5km), ignore a stile into a field on the left and continue for a further three quarters of a mile (1km) along the riverbank as far as the old paper mill. At the mill, turn right along the road and walk back to the Boat Inn (the inn usually serves food).

A Scenic Car Drive

Border Castles and Battlefields. 75 miles, ideally spent over at least two days as there is so much to see and explore on this drive through history.

The Borders and Northumbria are a land steeped in bloody history. Massive strongholds were built for the mighty and even more humble folk lived in fortified towers and bastles, where their animals were driven into the secure windowless ground floor with the families living above, safe from attack. The tour starts in **Berwick-upon-Tweed**, where the castle is all but swallowed by the railway station, but the massive town ramparts are the finest in Europe. From Berwick, follow the A698 south-west and divert to **Norham**, whose massive keep still guards a crossing over the Tweed. Return to the A698 and drive through Cornhill-on-Tweed to **Wark** on the B6350, whose castle was frequently besieged. Side roads off the A697 lead to Branxton and the **Battle of Flodden Field**, where a plaque and a granite cross are the memorial to the last and bloodiest battle in Northumberland, fought in 1513 between the English and Scots. About $1^{1}/_{2}$ miles to the east of the A697, the B6354 diverts to a Victorian adaptation of a medieval castle at **Ford**. Still following the A697, near Akeld at its junction with the B6351, a 'Bendor' stone marks the site of the **Battle of Homildon Hill** in 1402. (There is a bastle house at the head of Akeld village). Drive on through Wooler and take the B6348 then side roads to **Chillingham** where the restored medieval castle is set in attractive Italianate gardens. Follow side roads south from Chillingham and turn left along the B6346 to **Alnwick** (shops, hotels and restaurants), market town and seat of the Duke of Northumberland, whose castle still protects this once fortified town. Follow the B1340, north-east across the A1(T), and then by minor roads to the attractive fishing village of Craster; a short coastal walk, (see Selected Walks) leads to **Dunstanburgh Castle**, a Lancastrian stronghold during the Wars of the Roses. Using by-roads and the B1339, drive north to **Bamburgh** where the castle, once the capital of the Anglo-Saxon kingdom of Bernica, was restored by Lord Armstrong in the nineteenth century.

It will be necessary to use the A1(T) for the return to Berwick, but a diversion can be made beyond Fenwick to reach **Lindisfarne** (**Holy Island** — check tide conditions before crossing the causeway), where the tiny castle restored by Sir Edwin Lutyens in 1903, stands on an isolated pinnacle of dolerite.

2
TYNE AND WEAR

Newcastle upon Tyne is the vibrant commercial heart of the north-east, and makes a suitable starting point to describe the county of Tyne and Wear. From there the guide will cover its satellite towns, starting with those to the west and moving in a clockwise direction around the city to the coast. Towns south of the Tyne will be described before moving south down the A1(M) into the lower reaches of Weardale, and also covering the new towns and one time colliery villages on either side of the A19(T).

Until the nineteenth century, Newcastle was a medieval city. Then, by one of the finest examples of town planning of its day, it was altered into a distinguished place of solid northern buildings, with spacious streets and squares. The finest of these is Grey Street, one of the most elegant streets in Europe. Travellers arriving in Newcastle from the south, either by rail or road, will have a lasting impression of a city dominated by the graceful arch of the Tyne Bridge across the steep-sided valley. Once arrived, the best way to explore Newcastle is on foot and there is no better place to start than on the Old Quayside, the oldest part of the commercial city. A little way downstream of Tyne Bridge is the Trinity Maritime Centre, a group of restored ships' chandlers warehouses highlighted by an interesting maritime museum and function rooms on Broad Chare. Moving upstream towards the Swing Bridge, on the right is the Guildhall, an eighteenth-century adaptation of an earlier design by Robert Trollope. Inside the Guildhall is the hammerbeam-roofed Great Hall as well as the Merchant Adventurer's Court, still used for important civic occasions. Across the street is the stately group of houses known as Sandhill. At the end of the street is Castle Stairs leading to the South Postern, the last vestige of the Norman castle wall. On the right is the Moot Hall, and close by it is the County Hall.

The castle keep, on the left of County Hall, is separated from its main gate by the London to Edinburgh railway line. Most of the castle's stonework dates from 1172, but some of the battlements are embellishments, added by John Dobson during restoration work which followed the building of Central Station. On the north side of the castle, St Nicholas' Cathedral dates mainly from the fourteenth and fifteenth centuries and is notable for its 'Scottish Crown' lantern tower, one of two survivors of this style (the other is Edinburgh's St Giles Cathedral). Items of interest include the memorial to Admiral Lord Collingwood, and the magnificent brass eagle lectern of the early sixteenth century, the oldest in the North of England. Beneath the transept is a barrel-vaulted crypt, used as a charnel house in the Middle Ages. In the main body of the cathedral, a huge painting of the *Washing of the Disciples Feet'* dominates the back wall of the reredos. Several of the side chapel windows and also the east window contain fragments of medieval glass.

Stephenson's Monument stands at the head of Westgate Road opposite the station, a memorial to the major founding father of the railway system (1781-1848). Westgate follows the line of Hadrian's Wall, past Neville Hall and St John's Church, and the graceful Assembly Rooms near Finkle Street. West Walls, a restored section of the ancient city wall, leads to Stowell Street. Nearby is the Blackfriars Centre, on the site of an ancient monastery that dated from 1239. Further evidence of the city wall appears again and again, such as near the junction of Stowell Street and Newgate Street, where Grey's Monument acts as a guide back to the city centre.

Although the journey north along Northumberland Street is easy on foot, the one-way system has created a circuitous route for motorists. At its head is the modern administrative and shopping centre of Newcastle, with the Civic Centre and its dramatic statue of the Tyne god and the realistically sculptured *Swans in Flight*, both the work of the prize-winning artist David Wynal. Pedestrianised shopping streets fill the area between the Eldon Square opposite the Civic Centre and Grey Street.

Across Percy Street is the Newcastle University complex and the Museum of Antiquities which traces local history from 6000BC to 1600; on display are models of Hadrian's Wall, lifesized figures of Roman soldiers and a reconstructed Temple of Mithras. Other museums and galleries in the university precinct are: the Greek Museum in the Department of Classics; the Hatton Gallery, a collection of contemporary art, fifteenth-century paintings and collections of African sculpture. Other museums and art galleries can be found in nearby streets. The Hancock Museum, a collection of stuffed birds and animals, together with a geological gallery is on the Great North Road at Barras Bridge, while in Exhibition Park, off the Great North Road, is the Military Vehicle Museum. In nearby Turbina Hall is the *Turbina*, Charles Parson's graceful prototype steam turbine. The Science Museum is in Blandford Square, and contains much of the work of Newcastle's great engineers. The George Joicey Museum on City Road is a collection of military memorabilia, local history and period rooms in a seventeenth-century almshouse. Not far away from it on Sandwell, is Bessie Surtees House, developed from two sixteenth- and seventeenth-century merchants' houses, one half-timbered and the other refronted in brick about 1721. The principal rooms are on view and English Heritage, who use the house as their North Regional Headquarters, mount displays about the property and their work.

Town Moor is only a short distance north from the city centre. Each June the 'Hoppings' takes place, said to be one of the largest fairs in the country. Freemen of Newcastle still have the right to graze cattle on Town Moor. South of the ring road and a little way beyond the university, Leazes Park with its delightful terrace of houses built by Grainger, leads back to the city centre.

Newcastle is fortunate in having the unique geological feature of Jesmond Dene within easy reach of its commercial heart. The dene, to the north-east of the city centre, is a deep ravine cut through soft sandstone. It was once owned by Lord Armstrong, who gave it to the city about 100 years ago. Footpaths and a nature trail run through woodlands lining the river bank.

Downstream from Newcastle are densely populated **Byker** and **Walker**, and also the start of the Tyneside shipbuilding industry. In summer it is possible to take a ferry cruise of about $2^1/_2$ hours duration from the Old Quayside and see the shipbuilding at close hand. Moving west and upstream from Newcastle, then sweeping north and east above the city, the following paragraphs deal with the rest of Tyne and Wear north of the Tyne as far as the coast.

The industrial suburb of **Newburn** is built well above the north bank of the Tyne. George Stephenson, pioneer of the railway age, was twice married in the parish church of St Michael. Its tower and arcades are early Norman, and the chancel thirteenth-century. Lemington power station on the river bank, marks the place where the first steam locomotive *Puffing Billy* was built by William Hedley in 1813. It ran a full year before Stephenson's *Blücher*, hauling coal from Wylam Colliery. A collection of vintage cars of the 1920 to 1970s period is on display at the Newburn Hall Motor Museum in Townfield Gardens.

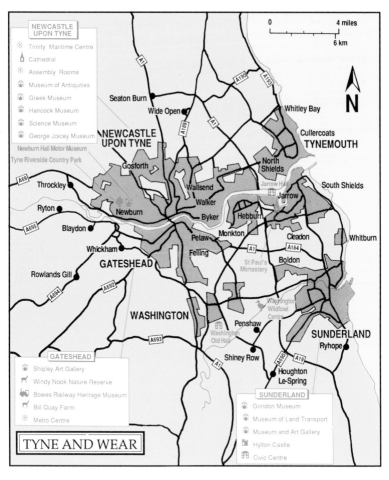

NEWCASTLE
UPON TYNE

Trinity Maritime Centre
Cathedral
Assembly Rooms
Museum of Antiquities
Greek Museum
Hancock Museum
Science Museum
George Joicey Museum
Newburn Hall Motor Museum
Tyne Riverside Country Park

GATESHEAD

Shipley Art Gallery
Windy Nook Nature Reserve
Bowes Railway Heritage Museum
Bill Quay Farm
Metro Centre

TYNE AND WEAR

SUNDERLAND

Grindon Museum
Museum of Land Transport
Museum and Art Gallery
Hylton Castle
Civic Centre

0   4 miles

6 km

N

Seaton Burn
Wide Open
Whitley Bay
NEWCASTLE
UPON TYNE
Cullercoats
TYNEMOUTH
Gosforth
North Shields
Throckley
Wallsend
Jarrow Hall
South Shields
Jarrow
Ryton
Walker
Newburn
Byker
Hebburn
Blaydon
Monkton
Pelaw
Cleadon
Whitburn
Whickham
Felling
Boldon
St Paul's Monastery
GATESHEAD
Rowlands Gill
Washington Wildfowl Centre
WASHINGTON
Penshaw
SUNDERLAND
Washington Old Hall
Ryhope
Shiney Row
Houghton Le-Spring

The Tyne Riverside Country Park stretches from Newburn to Wylam and is linked to **Throckley** by the Wylam and Walbottle Wagonway. This dormitory suburb spreads on either side of the A6085 about 6 miles west of Newcastle upon Tyne. The town has good views of the industrial lower reaches of the river and its main street follows the line of Hadrian's Wall; houses and shops on the south side of the street are actually built over the vallum. Small sections of the Wall and vallum can be seen on either side of the town.

Moving north-east around Newcastle, **Gosforth** is separated from

Newcastle upon Tyne

the city by Town Moor and Nun's Moor, and although very much a large residential suburb, it manages to convey something of its rural beginnings. Its most interesting feature is the 800-acre High Gosforth Park and racecourse, where the Northumberland Plate, the 'Pitman's Derby', is run every June. The park lake is home to wildfowl and is edged by dense woodland. Parts of the lake and the woodlands are designated as a Nature Reserve with large numbers of badgers, deer, woodland birds and waterfowl so near the Newcastle conurbations. Arrangements to visit the reserve can be made through the Natural History Society based at the Hancock Museum in Newcastle.

North for a couple of miles along the A1(T), strangely named **Wide Open** keeps itself aloof from the trunk road which divides it from its neighbour, Brunswick Village. **Seaton Burn**, the oldest of the group of interconnected villages, is to the north. The A1 Tyne Tunnel feeder road intersects the Great North Road, the A6125, about half a mile to the north. Woodland and water link these suburbs of Newcastle to farmland beyond the A1. Big Waters Nature Reserve has a $4^1/_2$ mile nature trail which is approached across the A6125 by a signposted lane from Seaton Burn.

Move south, and back towards the Tyne through a complex of

industrial suburbs to **Wallsend**, where as the name suggests, the eastern end of Hadrian's Wall can be found, or at least a small trace of it in the cleverly outlined plan of *Segedunum* Roman fort not far from the Swan Hunter shipyard (for further details, see Chapter 3).

The A1 takes a wide sweep to the east of Wallsend, missing out Newcastle and Gateshead to reach to Tyne Tunnel which surfaces between Howden Pans and Jarrow on the south side of the river.

The Stephenson Museum, a collection of rolling stock, includes *Killingworth Billy*, one of George Stephenson's early locomotives, built in 1826, together with *Silver Link* and other vintage railway engines. The Stephenson Trail traces the route of many of the old railway tracks and visits sites associated with him. It also visits **Killingworth** near Gosforth, the former colliery village where George Stephenson stayed when he was employed as an engineman at Killingworth Colliery. A sundial set into the wall of Dial Cottage, now a private residence, where Stephenson lived, is reputed to have been designed by him and carved by his son Robert. Stephenson's locomotive, *Blücher*, ran from the mine to the Tyne.

Shipyards and docks line the Tyne more or less all the way to the estuary. **North Shields** claims to be the birthplace of the steam trawler, a vessel which completely revolutionised the deep-sea fishing industry. A lively early morning fish market at Fish Quay (there is also a very competitive retail section), was first established by the monks of Tynemouth Priory. North Shields has a modern shopping centre and a cross-river passenger ferry service to South Shields. North Sea ferries sail from Willington Quay to Norway and Denmark. Smith's Dock, the largest ship repair dock on the Tyne, is close by.

A short riverside walk leads from Fish Quay to where Collinwood's massive statue guards the mouth of the Tyne. Guns surrounding the plinth came from the *Royal Sovereign*, his flagship at the Battle of Trafalgar. Nearby the Volunteer Life Brigade's Headquarters Watch House contains relics of ships wrecked along the coast, some as close as on the Black Middens, a notorious skerry below the priory.

Cullercoats fishwives no longer follow the herring fleets around the east coast, but they are commemorated by Wooden Dolly, a statue which once decorated a passageway leading to Fish Quay, but now stands in **Tynemouth**'s Northumberland Square. Part resort and part residential, the town is an interesting grouping of Victorian houses lining streets radiating from the central squares, many the one-time homes of sea captains.

On a headland above the river mouth, Tynemouth Priory, once a kind of penitentiary for recalcitrant monks, occupies the eastern cliffs. Linked to it on the shoreward side is a castle, built in the late thirteenth and fourteenth centuries to defend both priory and the river mouth; the gaunt ruins are now in the care of English Heritage. There is a museum in the old powder magazine, part of fortifications which were manned by gunners of the oldest volunteer artillery unit in the British army.

The holiday resort and residential town of **Whitley Bay** has all but swamped the old fishing village of Cullercoats, but fishing boats are still drawn up along the sandy shore. The sands attract holidaymakers or day trippers from the nearby industrial towns who come to enjoy the bracing sea air, or spend their money in the Spanish City amusement park. Promenade gardens, the Whitley Warriors, the town's own ice hockey team, and sea angling complete the ammenities.

South of the Tyne

Starting in the west, the first place along the county boundary is **Rowland's Gill**, a pleasant residential suburb built high above the wooded Derwent Valley, the boundary with County Durham. On the opposite side of the valley, the Derwent Walk Country Park is based on a railway track built in 1867. The park starts near Winlaton Mill outside Whickham and runs to Consett in the south-west. The route passes through 10 miles of woodland and unspoiled valley scenery, with many interesting features of the railway remaining.

The B6314, Burnopfield road crosses the Derwent valley below Rowland's Gill, giving access to **Gibside Chapel**, a Palladian-style mausoleum built for Sir George Bowes. This strangely compelling building was given to the National Trust in 1966 by the executors of the sixteenth Earl of Strathmore and Kinghorne. Beyond, and on private property, are the ruins of Gibside Hall. Architects such as James Paine, who designed the mausoleum, and landscape artist 'Capability' Brown were employed in the construction of the mansion and its parkland. Even though the hall is closed to the public, the statue of British Liberty, on top of its 140ft-tall column, can be seen from the Derwent Walk.

Downstream is **Blaydon**, an industrial town where Geordies used to go to the town's racecourse. Regretably, the last race on this course, immortalized by the Geordie 'national anthem' *Blaydon Races*, was in 1916; the Stella Power Station now occupies the site. To appreciate the town and its residential and older suburb **Winlaton**, you must climb the steep hillside above the A695. In Hood Square a chain forge has been preserved, part of a cottage industry which included nail making. Access to the forge may be arranged through the Winlaton Branch Library. Shibdon Pond Nature Reserve, near Blaydon, is a good place for bird watching.

Now move upstream along the Tyne to **Ryton**, a pretty place despite the proximity of Newcastle's bustling traffic. The small town stands above the south bank of the river and has grown southwards from its church, built on a pre-Christian religious site. Broach-spired Holy Cross Church dates from the thirteenth century and is built in the Early English style. It is noted for the Jacobean woodwork of its chancel screen and oak stalls. Ryton Willows is below the town, part of the Tyne Riverside Country Park which is based on a 2-mile long riverside footpath.

On the north side of the A69, is the **Metro Centre**, a massive complex of over 300 shops housed in spacious air-conditioned malls, accessible from 10,000 free car park spaces, or by frequent bus and railway services. Metroland, Europe's only indoor theme park is attached to the shopping facilities where all the family can take a break from shopping and enjoy the terrifying rides, or wander

Dial Cottage, Killingworth — home of George & Robert Stephenson

The Metro Centre, Gateshead

through 'mountain' scenery and admire the artificial waterfalls. A ten-screen cinema completes the amenities of the Metro which attracts customers from all over the North of England.

Urban and industrial sprawl continues all the way along the south bank of the Tyne to the coast, with **Gateshead** as its administrative centre. Its skyline is dominated by concrete tower blocks, but the oldest part of the town is built around St Mary's Church, itself dwarfed by the steel span of Tyne Bridge. The church was built in the Middle Ages, but most of the present building dates from the eighteenth and nineteenth centuries.

The town boasts a number of firsts, from its international sports stadium and nearby leisure centre to the Metro Centre. The arts are catered for with the Little Theatre at Saltwell View, and Caedmon Hall, in the Central Library complex, has programmes ranging from orchestral concerts to photographic exhibitions. Shipley Art Gallery has a permanent collection of paintings by Old Masters and Victorian artists.

Several areas of countryside are unexpectedly preserved within Gateshead's boundaries. Windy Nook Nature Reserve is to the south-east of the town while Bill Quay Farm on Hainingwood Terrace, off Shields Road, is an inner city farm containing many rare breeds. Bowes Railway Heritage Museum is near Springwell village south-east of Gateshead; access is from the A1(M)-A69 Birtley interchange. This unique museum is devoted to the only remaining standard gauge rope-hauled railway left in Britain. Audio-visual displays, exhibitions, locomotive workshops and steam hauled passenger trains complete the attractions.

Shipbuilding and heavy engineering on the south bank of the Tyne begin at **Hebburn**. Its industries are centred around the modernised Swan Hunter shipyards, once famous for building warships in the days of Britain's naval might. Dereliction upstream of the yards has been cleared and turned into an attractive marina and walkway. Backed by open grassland, it is a good place to watch the waterborne activities.

The site of St Bede's Well is to the south of Hebburn, at **Monkton** where the monks of Jarrow Priory are said to have drawn their water. Monkton is also the home of Hebburn Athletic Club, among whose members is the world-record-breaking middle distance runner, Steve Cram.

The ruins of the priory that Bede entered as a boy of 12 stand above the marsh of Jarrow Slake; these ruins, together with **Jarrow**'s parish church of St Paul, act as an island of tranquillity, surrounded on their landward side by oil storage tanks and paver lines; fortunately a low hill hides most of the industrial complex. This is where the Venerable Bede (673-735) wrote his ecclesiastical history of the English people. The oldest part remaining is the Saxon chapel at the east end built, it is thought around 681 with Roman stones. The tower dates from 1075 and is a curious mixture of styles within its four stages. A dedication stone which bears the date of St George's Day, 23 April 681, can be found above the tower arch.

A few hundred yards uphill across the pleasant green from the priory, Georgian Jarrow Hall, the oldest remaining house in the town, now serves as a museum dealing with relics from the priory and also as an information centre. Bede Gallery in Springwell Park on the other side of the town, holds regular exhibitions of contemporary art and the history of Jarrow.

Jarrow received fame in the 1930s when workers from its redundant shipyards marched on parliament, led by the town's redoubtable MP, Helen Wilkinson. The event is remembered by a plaque at the entrance to the Victorian town hall. Jarrow Riverside Park, with footpaths and views of modern shipyards, occupies reclaimed industrial land above the Tyne Tunnel.

The river meets the sea at **South Shields**, a town which grew around the Roman supply base of *Arbeia*. Part colliery town and part seaside resort, the modern town grew mostly in the nineteenth century. With the Victorian enthusiasm for sea and sand, the town's beaches at Littlehaven and Sandhaven soon attracted visitors from the nearby towns and from further afield. South Pier, the twin of one reaching out from Tynemouth, has created over a mile of excellent beach. Victorian terraced houses over the Roman fort have been demolished and foundations of buildings within the fort have been meticulously excavated and most of the site is now on display. Roman stones taken from redundant churches and old farms in the area have been used to reconstruct the imposing main gate. A simple, yet well laid out museum on site holds a number of important exhibits, including tombstones found on the site of a nearby Roman cemetery together with many well-preserved household objects.

The town's more recent past is commemorated in the town museum on Ocean Road, where there are displays of local archaeology and exhibits of the history of shipbuilding, especially lifeboats. The first lifeboat, aptly called the *Original*, was invented by two South Shields men, Henry Greathead and William Wouldhave; their memorial, a preserved lifeboat, is on a street corner near Marine Park. A special gallery is devoted to Catherine Cookson who was born close by and has based most of her romantic novels on Tyneside and Northumbrian life. There is a Catherine Cookson trail which follows her early life and career around South Tyneside. Details can be obtained from local tourist offices.

Coastal scenery south of the Tyne soon develops from wide sandy beaches to high limestone cliffs, the haunt of sea birds. Several 'stacks', or isolated rocks, with Marsden Rock the most prominent, are nesting places for a wide range of the birds and the whole of this section of coastline is classified as a site of special scientific interest and a nature reserve. Constant erosion by the sea makes the cliffs dangerous and they should not be climbed. *Take heed of the warning notices*.

Marsden Bay is a popular beach reached by steps or a lift from the car park near Velvet Beds. The Grotto, an unusual and unexpected public house and restaurant is on the beach at the foot of the steep flight of steps. It is built into the cliff and was originally the home of a local character by the name of Jack the Blaster, who carved a home for himself and his family out of the cliff in 1782. Subsequent owners extended the cave dwelling into a fifteen-roomed house which became this unusual pub. Cave dwelling people with odd names seem to have been a feature of the bay; characters with names like Willie the Rover and Dolly Jim, have all lived in and around the cliffs of Marsden Bay. Smuggling was a popular occupation and the cliff

Marsden Rock

caves offered privacy to anyone wanting to keep themselves hidden from authority. A red and white candy-striped lighthouse on Lizard Point marks the southern limit of Marsden Bay.

Just around the corner from Lizard Point and set back from a rocky beach is **Whitburn**, a neat and tidy village with a sloping green surrounded by houses of character and a spacious main street. Whitburn has become mostly residential since its colliery closed. The church, with its narrow buttressed tower, is Early English, dating from the thirteenth century, but with later addtions and restoration. Whitburn Hall, a mixture of styles from the seventeenth century onwards, stands enclosed in its own gardens south-west of the town centre. Sandy Whitburn Bay separates the village from its big brother Sunderland a short distance to the south.

Cleadon and Boldon are a couple of miles inland, a slight rise of the land to the north-east is known as the Cleadon Hills, where the carving of a white horse is in memory of a young woman who was last seen riding her white mare along the beach near Marsden Rock and who was presumed to have been swept out to sea. A golf course and a windmill are the other features of these hills.

Grotto Inn, Marsden Bay

Washington Old Hall

Sunderland and the Lower Wear

Sunderland, at the mouth of the Wear, was once the largest ship-building town in the world, but despite the changes to modern methods, its shipyards have continued to see massive redundancies. Downstream from the yards, twin curved stone piers protect the harbour mouth, a popular place for sea angling, and the inshore rescue lifeboat is based on the north side below Roker pier. Sandy beaches stretch on either side of the estuary; those to the north are the best and most accessible. Two bridges cross the Wear, taking traffic from Monkwearmouth and Southwick into the town centre. Queen Alexandra Bridge built in 1909, is upstream. Originally double-decked carrying both rail and road traffic, it gives pedestrians a good vantage point above the modern shipyards of Pallion and Southwick. Wearmouth Bridge dates from 1929 and spans the river with massive steel arches carrying the A1018 into the modernized town centre. Sturdy Victorian and Edwardian commercial properties surround the modern part and Georgian town houses can still be recognized.

St Peter's Church stands in a green oasis on the north side of the river. Sunderland's oldest building, it was founded in AD674 and has links with the Venerable Bede. Originally part of a monastery, the oldest and Saxon part of the church is in the west end. The chancel is fourteenth century, but the rest of the church dates from a Victorian restoration.

Several imaginative museums devote themselves to Sunderland's industrial past. Grindon Museum to the south-west of the town centre, is furnished with Edwardian rooms and shop interiors. Monkwearmouth station is now the Museum of Land Transport, and has been faithfully restored as it was in its Edwardian heyday, with displays of rolling stock and the development of locomotives. Sunderland Museum and Art Gallery is devoted to the wildlife and geology of the North-East; also the history of shipbuilding, pottery and glass making in the area. Period rooms, displays of silver and exhibitions of paintings fill other galleries. The North-East Aircraft Museum is at Sunderland Airport.

A civic theatre trust has preserved the Edwardian opulence of the Empire Theatre, while a still-functioning windmill beside the Newcastle road at Fulwell, is the only complete survivor of many which dotted the North-East. The remains of fifteenth-century Hylton Castle are on the western outskirts of the town and consist mainly of the impressive gatehouse tower, the entrance to what was probably a simple rectangular tower-keep. Built by William de Hylton, the castle is supposed to be haunted by the 'Cauld Lad of Hylton'.

The Civic Centre is opposite Mowbray Park. Designed by the Sir Basil Spence, Bonnington and Collins Partnership, it is built from hexagonal blocks and surrounds open courts. Sports facilities in the area range from sailing and waterskiing to indoor amenities at the Crowtree Leisure Centre, where there is a leisure pool with a hydroslide, ice rink, sports facilities, indoor bowling and a summer playpark. Ferry trips along the Wear to the Washington Wildfowl Centre, and a dry ski slope on reclaimed colliery land at Silksworth, complete the amenities. Sunderland illuminations are becoming an established feature each autumn.

A little to the south of Sunderland and separated from the sea by the coast-hugging Sunderland to Hartlepool railway, the colliery village of **Ryhope** has one of the finest monuments of Victorian steam engineering ability in the North-East. Ryhope Pumping Engine was designed to lift water from wells deep below the ground. The 1868 pumping station is about a mile inland along the Warden Law road. Superseded by reservoir supplies, it has been carefully restored and is open most weekends, being steam operated on bank holidays. A small museum on the site follows the development of pumped water supplies throughout the ages.

Moving inland, the A182 Hartlepool to Washington road separates the twin colliery villages of **Shiney Row** and **Penshaw**. Both are straggling places of miners' cottages and red-brick estates, overlooking the woodlands of Lambton Park and an inland stretch of the Wear before it flows through its final and industrial estuary. Penshaw church is mock-Norman, built in 1830 and containing, of all things, a stone from the Great Pyramid of Egypt. Dominating the skyline to the north-east is Penshaw Monument, a fanciful Grecian temple, built not as the Parthenon on solid rock, but on a scrub-covered hillock; as a result it looks better from afar. A waymarked circular walk of about $3^1/_2$ miles links Penshaw Monument to both natural and industrial features above the nearby River Wear. The monument is owned and maintained by the National Trust. **Lambton Castle**, basically a nineteenth-century creation which was used for a time as a teacher-training college, is strictly within County Durham, but its links are closer to the towns and villages of Tyne and Wear to its north and east. It is a green oasis hemmed in by traffic on the A1 motorway and the A182. There is a caravan site here.

Washington, one of the most successful new towns in the North East, was created in 1967 and is still developing. Intended to attract industry into a declining colliery area, it has brought international companies and Government offices into this hitherto depressed part of Tyne and Wear. The town plan deliberately segregates motor vehicles from pedestrians, and as a result can be rather confusing to first-time visitors. Signposts direct motorists to areas described by district numbers, none of which can be seen from roads that are mostly confined to cuttings. However, once away from the road the pattern becomes clear and instead of an impersonal town of up to 80,000 inhabitants, each district has developed its own self-contained village atmosphere. Most of the well-designed houses are set in green fields on high ground above the River Wear. Streams and trees have been preserved in an attempt to create natural settings whenever possible, all adding to the rapidly growing maturity of the town.

Washington is built around the unspoilt nucleus of the old village, where seventeenth-century Washington Old Hall, a National Trust property, has become a place of pilgrimage to visiting Americans. The Stars and Stripes of the United States of America is proudly flown the flagpole in front of the hall, proclaiming what is a doubtful link between this part of Britain and America. The hall was certainly owned by the Washington family until the thirteenth century, but there is no proof that George Washington ever visited it. He lived at Sulgrave in Northamptonshire before emigrating to America. Despite these rather tenuous historical links, Washington Hall is worth visiting in its own right. Mainly a Jacobean manor house, it has some excellent panelling and an oak staircase. Parts, especially the kitchen, date from the original thirteenth-century house. Souvenirs of George Washington are on display in rooms set aside for the purpose.

Mining has completely vanished from the area; the only relic is 'F' Pit Mining Museum on Albany Way, to the north of the town and signposted from the A1231. The original shaft was sunk in 1777, making this the oldest working pit in Britain before it closed in 1968. The winding house and the magnificent 1888 steam winding engine, the last of its type in the North-East, are on display. Washington has a thriving arts centre at Biddick Farm, Fatfield. Housed in traditional nineteenth-century farm buildings, the centre offers a wide range of exhibitions and performances.

The Wildfowl and Wetlands Centre is based on a riverside Nature Reserve off the A1231, to the east of the town. Developed on reclaimed industrial land, the centre, with its 100 acres of ponds and woods on land sloping to the River Wear, has become a haven for visiting wildfowl. A viewing gallery, access for the disabled, hides, picnic areas and feeding facilities (especially for the flock of Chilean flamingoes, each individually named after a Catherine Cookson character) make this an interesting place to visit.

3
HADRIAN'S WALL

B y AD90, Rome had virtually conquered the whole of southern Britain and the country was settling down under its new masters, but further advance north was hindered by the warlike tribes, notably the Picts, who could carry out guerilla attacks under the cover offered by their wild mountains and glens. Such harassment on Rome's far northern frontier, not only in Britain but elsewhere, began to stretch the conqueror's military and administrative resources. In order to mark these northern limits of the Roman Empire, lines of forts and later walls were built in the northern part of the Black Forest region of Germany, across the narrow neck of land between the Rhine and the Danube. In Britain the conveniently narrow neck of land between present-day Newcastle and Carlisle, with the north facing crags of the Whin Sill at its central point, offered an ideal route for a defensive system marking Rome's north-west frontier.

Originally this frontier was a line of forts, such as the one at *Vindolanda* between Once Brewed and Bardon Mill, connected by Stanegate and following a route roughly parallel to and south of the eventual position of the Wall. A decision to strengthen them by a wall was made soon after Emperor Hadrian's visit to Britain in 122. His wall had until recently something of a modern counterpart in the Berlin Wall which marked the East-West divide. Like the Berlin Wall, it was a means of delineating a frontier between two ideologies, of controlling movement both north as well as south, and acting as a customs or trade barrier. Unlike the rapidly disappearing Berlin Wall, Hadrian's Wall has stood the test of time, and despite the robbing of its stone for convenient building material, large stretches of it are still recognisable more than eighteen hundred years after its construction.

The actual work of building what became known as Hadrian's Wall was carried out under the control of a military engineer called Aulus Platorious Nepos. He planned that it should stretch 80 Roman miles (about 74 modern miles, 119km), from *Pons Aelius* (on the site of modern Newcastle upon Tyne) to *Maia* (Bowness-on-Solway). The width was to be 10 Roman feet (one Roman foot equals 11.7in) and its height about 15ft, rising to a 6ft high battlemented parapet backed by a walkway. Along its front, about 20ft to the north, was a broad, deep ditch only omitted where steep crags or the sea made it unnecessary. Milecastles, as the name suggests, were spaced equidistantly one Roman mile apart, to provide both defensive cover and habitation for troops stationed along the Wall. Between each milecastle, two turrets, again spaced evenly, defenced the intervening length of Wall. As a means of strengthening the Wall's defending forces, extra forts, such as the one at *Vercovium* which is better known today as Housesteads, were built on or close to the Wall. Those forts to the south of the Wall, such as *Vindolanda* which formed part of the original defensive line, garrisoned support troops, and because of their comparative safety, became places where forward troops spent their leave and also civilian settlements grew beneath their protection. To the south of the Wall, at distances which vary between a few yards and half a mile, a complex ditch known as the vallum was dug some years later. The vallum was basically a deep ditch with a single high mound to its north and two lower ones to the south. The true use of this structure is not clear, but popular theories suggest that it was either designed as the southern boundary of the military zone around the Wall, into which only soldiers or people with special permits were allowed to go; or it could have been a fiendish means of trapping anyone who had breached the Wall. Whatever its purpose, the vallum, several years younger than the Wall, was probably considered unnecessary in later years. Crossings were made in it during more settled times and it was eventually abandoned. To aid rapid troop movements, a narrow road — still clearly visible in many places, even serving as a public right of way near Steel Rigg — was built immediately south of the Wall, and was the final stage in this massive undertaking.

A current theory suggests that the finished Wall was coated with whitewash. This would serve a triple purpose: to preserve the mortar binding the stones and to outline anyone standing near it; but mainly to create an awesome spectacle when viewed from the north. Not only was there a high wall manned by highly trained soldiers, but its ditch defences on the north side had to be crossed, or the crag climbed, before the Wall could be scaled, and afterwards the vallum would trap the unwary. Unlike the Maginot Line in modern history Hadrian's Wall was very difficult to bypass, and recent research suggests that a line of coastal forts in the west continued beyond the end of the Wall at *Maia* (Bowness-on-Solway), and on towards St Bees Head in Cumbria.

Hadrian's Wall was built in sections by detachments seconded from the three legions based in the area. Each legion was responsible for its own length, which in turn was broken into sub-sections, alloted to individual centuries of troops, who often left carved centurial stones to mark their work. Despite their obvious skills in building a wall that has lasted over 1,800 years, their survey methods were not of the highest quality; several sub-sections of the Wall have 'butted' joints which are several inches out of line, a number of which can be seen on a walk along the Wall from Steel Rigg towards Housesteads fort.

Once the actual construction of the Wall began, lack of convenient stone prevented its being built to the planned width of 10 Roman feet; many sections remain narrow, but on a wide base. In other places, especially to the west of *Camboglana*, at Birdoswald (Cumbria) near Gilsland, the Wall had to be made from turf when stone was in short supply, although later, many sections of this turf wall were rebuilt in stone.

When finished, Hadrian's Wall needed about 13,000 troops to defend it, many of them based in the extra forts built to accommodate them. In more peaceful times, civilian settlements grew alongside the protection of the forts where retired soldiers married local women and set up home. Tradesmen and inn-keepers moved in to supply the needs of the civilians and off-duty soldiers. Small farms developed on the southern slopes beneath the protection of the Wall. Their carefully contrived terraces can still be seen in places, such as on the sides of the dry valley opposite Housesteads fort; aqueducts, skillfully following contour lines to provide fresh water to the forts, can still be traced for several miles across the northern moors. A good example is the aqueduct which carried water from Grenlee Lough below Housesteads to *Aesica* fort at Great Chesters, about 6 miles further west. Customs posts were established to monitor the flow of trade and movement of people north and south in times of peace. There is an excellent example of one of these gateways where the Wall crosses Knag Burn immediately north-east of Housesteads fort.

In less settled times, Hadrian's Wall was breached many times by attackers from the north, the major defeats being in 197, 300 and 367, but the Roman withdrawal is usually considered to have taken place about 409.

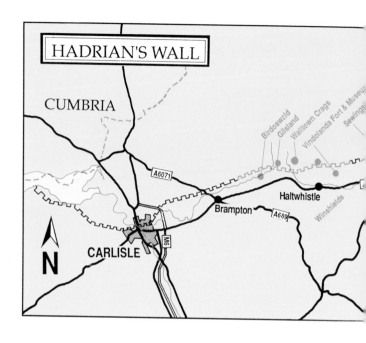

Hadrian's Wall; a detail of the stonework

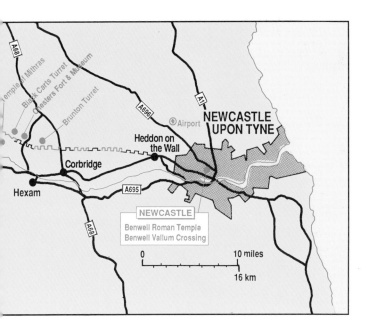

Part of the wall which runs along the top of the Whin Sill at Cuddy's Crags

When the troops withdrew from England, Roman law and order broke down as Scots, Angles and Saxons invaded the north, many of them eventually settling and becoming respectable farmers, but many centuries were to pass before anyone could go about their peaceful business in any degree of safety. Although people lived within the comparative shelter of the abandoned forts for another 1,300 years, Hadrian's Wall gradually fell into disrepair. Its stones became ready-made building material for local churches and farmhouses in the area. The section of the Wall near Housesteads owes its preservation to the fact that for many years a notorious band of moss-troopers, Border rievers, used the remains of the fort as their headquarters. The final act of vandalism occurred when General Wade built the Military Road (B6318), from Heddon-on-the-Wall, on the western outskirts of Newcastle upon Tyne, to Carlisle, during the 1715 Jacobite Rebellion. The road follows the line of the Wall for much of its length, especially in the east where it is built over it. Despite the protests of many eighteenth-century archaeologists, Wade's roadbuilders used the convenient stone from the Wall for their foundations. Before the B6318 was metalled, it was possible to make out the oblong blocks of wallstones; and many still lie buried beneath the modern surface.

In more enlightened times work began on preserving what was left of Hadrian's Wall and also excavating its forts. What remains is an exciting link with Roman Britain. Even though there are few places where the ruins are more than an outline of a building's foundations, or perhaps only part of the final height of the Wall, it does not need much imagination to see them as they were when the Romans left. Museums and carefully reconstructed towers and gateways such as at *Arbeia* in South Shields, or on the *Vindolanda* site, help to appreciate this massive undertaking.

With the aid of the excellent strip map of Hadrian's Wall published by the Ordnance Survey, it is possible to follow most of it on the ground. However, care should be taken not to trespass where the Wall crosses private land. At the time of writing, plans are being made to create a long distance footpath which will follow the route of Hadrian's Wall from coast to coast. While there is much that the inexperienced visitor to Hadrian's Wall can see and begin to understand and appreciate, there are still large sections where forts and other buildings, or even the line of the Wall itself, are only apparent as grassy mounds or piles of stones. These are the realm of the trained archaeologist, but there is still an amazing amount of detail available to the interested observer. The following list gives details of those sites on and close by the Wall, and of nearby forts and townships associated with the military zone surrounding the Wall. Most are accessible to the general public, but in the rare case where a site is on private land, such as at Written Crag which is a little to one side of a public footpath, or the stretch of the vallum near the road at Limestone Corner, the landowner's permission must be sought before gaining access. The list follows the Wall from east to west, and includes those sites in Cumbria which are outside the normal scope of this guide.

Accessible Sites Associated with Hadrian's Wall

The Roman name, where known, is in brackets.

South Shields (*Arbeia*)
Signposted from town centre.

Supply port and guard-fort for the southern arm of the mouth of the Tyne. Almost completely excavated; reconstructed main gate. Small, but interesting museum containing many of the personal belongings of soldiers who guarded the fort, or of people who lived in the nearby township.

Wallsend (*Segedunum*)
Buddle Street and roadside features near the town centre.

The most easterly point of Hadrian's Wall, built after it was found that the original ending of the Wall at *Pons Aelius* (Newcastle upon Tyne), was vulnerable to attack. Parts of towers, the headquarters building and a small section of the Wall are visible. The rest of the fort is outlined by coloured flagstones and gravel in a town centre park, a reclamation of Victorian terraced streets near Swan Hunter's shipyards.

Benwell (*Condercum*)
Roadside A69
Preserved gateway stones and foundations of a temple.

Denton Burn
Roadside A69
Part of Turret 7B and 55yd of Wall. Short stretch of the vallum beyond a housing estate, a little to the south-west of the main road, has three clearly defined crossings.

Heddon-on-the-Wall
Roadside B6528
110yd of Wall and rock-cut vallum to the east of the village and further sections of vallum and fore-ditch to the north-west.

Vindolanda — *the* mansio *(inn)*

Vindolanda — *the hypocaust or underfloor heating system at the Bath House*

Housesteads Fort

Wallhouses
Near junction of B6318 and B6321
2 miles of fore-ditch and about a
mile of vallum with crossings.

Halton Shields
Roadside B6318
About a mile of vallum.

Corbridge *(Corstopitum)*
South of A69(T) and A68, about
half a mile west of the village.

Important Roman town about
$2^1/_2$ miles south of the Wall; supply base, adminstrative centre
and rear echelon garrison town.
Still only partly excavated, but
work to date indicates the size
and importance of the town.
Comprehensive museum on site.
Owned and maintained by English Heritage.

Walkers at Housesteads

Whittington Fell

Roadside B6318 between the A68 roundabout and Heavenfield church at Hill Head.

Over 3 miles of vallum and fore-ditch. Short lengths of the Roman Military Way and the foundations of Milecastle 23.

Written Crag Roman Quarry

Fallowfield Fell; reached by footpath south of B6318, map reference NY938686.

Site of Roman quarry where one of the workmen carved the inscription *Petra Flavi Carantini* 'the rock of Flavius Carantinus'. The inscription is now in Chesters Museum, but the quarry is recognisable.

Chesters *(Cilurnum)*

B6318 Chollerford

Excavated site of a Wall fort garrisoned by a cavalry unit. Many important buildings uncovered, including the headquarters building and its strong room; commandant's house, and an extensive bath-house, where the garrison enjoyed their relaxation. Remains of bridge abutment over the North Tyne. Extensive museum; maintained by English Heritage.

Limestone Corner

Map Reference NY876716. Roadside B6318.

Foreditch unfinished due to hardness of rock; loose boulders apparently left in situ when the site was abandoned. Over 2 miles of roadside vallum with numerous crossing points on either side of Limestone Corner. *NB Take care if parking at the side of this road.*

Carrawburgh *(Brocolitia,* or *Procolitia)*

B6318, 3 miles west of Chollerford

Partly excavated Wall fort, built over, and therefore later than the vallum. Only grassy mounds indicate the plan of this yet to be fully rediscovered fort. Interesting remains, a few yards to the south-west, of a Mithraic temple. About 3ft of the temple's outer wall remains, and upright concrete posts indicate the position of internal roof supports. Replicas of three altars, (the originals are in Chesters Museum near Chollerford), stand at the north end of the aisle. About 500ft to the north-west along a boggy ditch is the site of Coventina's Well, a sacred spring where an attractive plaque set up by a cohort of Batavians, together with numerous coins and other votive offerings now in Chesters Museum, was found.

The vallum interspersed by crossing points is clearly visible, running parallel to the B6318 for several miles between Carrawbrugh and Once Brewed. *NB Take great care when negotiating the blind crests along this stretch of the B6318.*

Housesteads *(Vercovicium)*
B6318 about $2^1/_2$ miles north-east of Once Brewed.

Extensively excavated site of a Wall fort, garrisoned from 200 by the 1,000-strong First Cohort of Tungrians (who came from what is now Belgium). Foundations of most of the principal buildings including the *Principa*, or headquarters building, the *Praetorium*, or commandant's house, granaries, and perimeter wall are clearly defined; of special interest is the complex latrine near the southern gate *(Porta Principalis Dextra)*. Notice also the well-worn and wheel-rutted threshold stones in the east gate *(Porta Praetoria)*, and the large stone water-tank near the partially blocked north gate *(Porta Principalis Sinistra)*. A gateway where the Wall crosses Knag Burn immediately to the north-west of the fort marks the site of a customs post, and a well can just be made out about 100yd downstream along the burn. Terraces on the hillsides south of the fort indicate the extensive civilian settlement which built up around Housesteads. The site is run jointly by the National Trust and English Heritage. An information centre at the roadside car park, run jointly by the National Trust and the Northumberland National Park, along with a museum next to the fort, help to explain the history of this best-preserved site on Hadrian's Wall.

Access from the car park is along a short, well-made path which is steep in places. There is a car park for the disabled next to the museum; enquire at the National Trust/National Park car park on the B6318.

Steel Rigg
About $^3/_4$ mile north of Once Brewed (B6318).

The best preserved and scenically most attractive part of the Wall is the $3^1/_2$ mile section south-west from Housesteads Fort to Steel Rigg car park. Follows the escarpment of the Whin Sill crag and includes the clearly defined foundations of Milecastle 39 (NY760677). Good stretch of the vallum can be seen over the roadside wall (B6318) opposite the Once Brewed Information Centre. (See the recommended walk which covers the best features of Hadrian's Wall. Details at the end·of this chapter).

The Bath House, Chesters

Chesterholme *(Vindolanda)*

$1^1/_2$ miles north of Bardon Mill (A69).

$3^1/_2$-acre site of rear echelon fort south of the Wall, and civilian settlement built in the third century to replace an earlier, mainly wooden group of buildings. Originally part of the line of forts which defended the northern frontier before Hadrian's Wall was built. Foundations of most of the principal buildings and a complex military bath house have been well excavated and many of the finds, including personal items such as footwear and parts of uniforms can be seen in the site museum. A large *Mansio*, or inn, and extensive workshops indicate the size of the civilian settlement.

Part of the site has been used to display reconstructed examples of both the stone and turf Wall at their full height, together with towers and military hardware such as *ballisti* (large stone-throwing catapults).

The site is run by the Vindolanda Trust based on Chesterholme House. The trust welcome volunteers to help with the on-going excavations of the site every summer.

Chesterholme, Stanegate
Used as the access lane to the *Vindolanda* site, off the Bardon Mill to Once Brewed road.

A Roman road linking forts to the south of Hadrian's Wall. Two Roman mileposts are sited on the north side of the lane, one near its junction with the Bardon Mill to Once Brewed road, the other in the garden of Chesterholme.

The outlines of 'marching forts', or temporary encampments, can be seen to the west of the road.

Winshields Crag
(NY745676), $^1/_2$ mile north-west of Once Brewed Information Centre.
Highest point on Hadrian's Wall, 1,230ft above sea level.

Cawfields Crag
(NY716667), off B6318, $1^1/_2$ miles north of Haltwhistle.
$^3/_4$ mile of repaired Wall and well preserved Milecastle 42.

Great Chesters *(Aesica)*
(NY705668), at the side of a public footpath near Great Chesters Farm, $1^1/_2$ miles north of Haltwhistle.

Fragmentary remains of partly excavated Wall fort. Fore-ditch, Wall and Roman Military Way are clearly visible.

Another view of the Chesters site

Carvoran *(Banna)*
$^1/_2$ mile east of Greenhead, (B6318).
Partly excavated site of small fort $^1/_4$ mile south of the Wall.

Walltown Crags
(NY674664), 1 mile north-east of Greenhead (B6318).
400yd of Wall and out-of-sequence turret pre-dating the Wall and thought to have been a signal station.

Thirwall Castle
$^1/_2$ mile north of Greenhead, B6318.
Fourteenth-century castle built from stones taken from Hadrian's Wall, a little over a hundred yards to the south.

Gilsland
(NY632662), B6318, 5 miles north-west of Haltwhistle.
   220yd of narrow wall built on wide base to conserve stone. In garden of former vicarage on unclassified road south of the centre of Gilsland.
Bridge abutment and sparse foundations of a water mill, to the east of the present course of the River Irthing.
Foundations of Milecastles 48 and 49 together with intervening turrets on either side of the river.

The following sites are in Cumbria:

Birdoswald *(Camboglanna)*
(NY616663), minor road off the B6318, $1^1/_2$ miles west of Gilsland.
   Oblong cavalry wall fort built on the site of an earlier signal station, itself built over an ancient British settlement. Good examples of gateways, outer walls, foundations of the headquarters building, granaries, barracks and a series of ovens near the south gateway.
   The fort was built on the line of the stone Wall which replaced an earlier turf Wall a few hundred yards to its south. The outline of the turf Wall and part of the vallum are on private land about a mile to the south-west of the fort. Turrets 51A and 51B and the tallest section of the Wall are at the side of the minor road, 2 miles south-west of Birdoswald.

Pike Hill Signal Tower
(NY577648), south of minor road east of Banks village, $3^1/_2$ miles north-east of Brampton.
   Foundations of 20ft-square Roman signal tower, placed at an angle of 45 degrees to the Wall.

Bank's East Turret
(NY575647), south of minor road, east of Banks village.
Well-preserved 'Turf Wall' turret.

NB The line of Hadrian's Wall continues westwards past Carlisle to
the Irish Sea at Bowness-on-Solway, but being mainly built of turf, it
is only obvious as occasional humps and hollows in fields along its
line.

A Walk Along Hadrian's Wall

$7^1/_2$ miles (12km). Moderate walking, but needs all day!
Map: Ordnance Survey Landranger Series, 1:50000 Scale. Sheet No
87: Hexham and Haltwhistle.

This walk follows the best preserved and most interesting section of
Hadrian's Wall, with a visit to the Wall fort of *Vercovicium* at
Housesteads and *Vindolanda* settlement. Take as much time as you
wish; the whole day will be necessary to appreciate the many and
varied things to see along the way. The walk starts from the National
Park Information Centre at Once Brewed on the B6318. There is a car
park and a summer-only bus service from Bardon Mill on the A69,
access by rail from Newcastle or Carlisle.

*Before setting out on the walk, visit the small, but informative museum
attached to the information centre. It will give you a greater understanding
of the way people have lived in the area around Hadrian's Wall, both before
and after it was built.*

Cross the B6318 (watch out for speeding traffic), and walk up the lane
opposite as far as Steel Rigg car park.

*Look over the boundary walls right and left of the junction of the lane and
the B6318; the ditch-like mounds are the remains of the vallum, a defensive
ditch which was built to the rear of the Wall, but later abandoned.*

Turn right and walk through the car park, then climb the stile and
turn left to follow Hadrian's Wall for about $2^1/_2$ miles (4km) to
Housesteads Fort.

*When completed, Hadrian's Wall stood about 15ft high to a 6ft parapet; in
some places, but not along its full length, it was about 10ft wide and built
from locally quarried stone. Built in sections by different military units,
many are several inches out of line. The path follows the Wall across Peel*

Crags and in a depression known as Castle Nick are the carefully excavated foundations of Milecastle 39. Eighty of these milecastles, holding up to sixty-four soldiers and spaced a Roman mile apart, guarded the Wall from Segedunum *(Wallsend) to* Maia *(Bowness-on-Solway); each had two turrets spaced equidistantly on either side where four soldiers patrolled their section of the wall.*

The section of Wall is missing beyond Milecastle 39. Scramble on to Highshields Crag for the view of Crag Lough, a natural tree-lined lake at the foot of the dolerite cliff.

Bear right away from the top of the crag to follow a narrow, but obviously man-made path. This is the Roman Military Way, which served as a speedy means of communication along the Wall. Follow the path until it reaches an access lane to Hotbank Farm. Cross this and walk uphill until the Military Way rejoins the Wall.

There is a good view looking backward to Crag Lough near Hotbank Farm. There are a few traces of the Wall here, and one cannot help wondering how many of its stones were used to build the farm.

Climb again towards a small plantation and go to the left of the wind-blown trees to reach a well preserved section of Hadrian's Wall. Follow this into Rapishaw Gap then climb across Cuddy's Crags, past the remains of Milecastle 37 to reach Housesteads Fort.

A signpost in Rapishaw Gap indicates the route of the Pennine Way long distance footpath from Edale in Derbyshire, which turns north at this point towards its final stages into Scotland.

Turn right and climb down into Housesteads Fort. Most of the excavated buildings are named, but you might prefer to obtain the site guide-book from the museum before exploring any further.

Wander down the 'main street', the Via Principalis, *or look out for the well-rutted stones beneath the gateways. Cleanliness and sanitation were of great importance in Roman life; the complex channels which feed clean water to the latrine near the south gate can still be seen.*

Before leaving the site, follow the Roman Military Way out of the east gate and down into the shallow valley of Knag Burn. A small gate where the path regains the Wall was a customs post, controlling movement of animals, goods and people, both north and south of the Wall.

Walk down to the museum (where you should pay the entrance fee to look round Housesteads), have a look at the model of the fort and items found during archaeological digs. Go through the gate behind the museum and walk down the surfaced lane as far as the main road.

Take care when crossing the B6318. Climb the ladder stile opposite and follow the narrow footpath across the dry valley to climb the far hillside. Walk across an undulating stretch of rough grazing, then go downhill towards the farmhouse of East Grindledykes.

Keep to the left of the farm buildings and cross a shallow valley by the farm's access drive. Turn right on reaching a road and continue around a steep hillside. Keep left at the next road junction.

The road follows the route of Stanegate, the Roman road linking the line of east-west forts that pre-date Hadrian's Wall. Stanegate is Old English for 'stone road', the Roman title being unknown. It runs from the supply base of Corstopitum *outside modern Corbridge to* Petriana *across the river from* Luguvalium, *modern Carlisle.*

A Roman signal station was built on the site of an ancient British settlement at the highest point on the left of the road.

Follow the road downhill towards a valley and look out for a signpost directing traffic into the *Vindolanda* car park. Turn right and go down the lane, past a Roman milestone, to Chesterholme, a beautiful house surrounded by attractive gardens and now the *Vindolanda* museum.

Look through the museum before venturing out on to the site of the Roman fort, as it will make everything simpler to understand.

The fort, which held about 500 troops, was part of the back-up system of the northern defences. The garrison lived in some style, as witness the complex bath-house and extensive commandant's house. Retired soldiers and civilians lived around the fort; some must have been fairly well off, if the size of their houses is anything to go by. Workshops have been found and an inn, or Mansio, *uncovered.*

Sections of Hadrian's Wall and full-size models of military equipment have been built to one side of the excavated fort.

The final $1^1/_2$ miles back to Once Brewed are along a road, but you can miss this in summer by using the bus which serves most of the archaeological sites in the area.

If walking, follow the access lane away from *Vindolanda* and turn right on reaching the Bardon Mill road. Follow this back to Once Brewed.

The road walk is not without its interest. There was a Roman cemetary in a field beyond Causeway House, which is on the right of the Vindolanda access lane. Further along the lane, again on the right, a stone column was a Roman milestone, still in its original position on Stanegate.

As you walk along the last stretch of road towards Once Brewed, look out for ridges on the hillside above Brackies Burn. These are the remains of the outer walls of temporary, or marching, camps built by Roman soldiers when travelling in an area without suitable accommodation. Turf ramparts were quickly thrown up in the traditional square or oblong design of all Roman forts and the soldiers would pitch their leather tents in an ordered pattern with the commanding officer's tent in the middle. The layout was exactly the same as in stone forts and each soldier could find the exact position of his tent even in the dark.

4
COUNTY DURHAM

County Durham is divided into three distinctly different regions. Its western boundary, now part of an Area of Outstanding Natural Beauty, is high on the wild Pennine moors, drained by its two major and contrasting valleys, Weardale and Teesdale, which flow into the second region, the industrial hinterland, which only finishes at the coast. Christianity's roots are deep in the soil of County Durham, a link which culminates in the glory of Durham Cathedral and a city whose medieval foundations are clearly visible in modern administrative centre and university city, the third region in this county of contrasts.

Durham City

The first and most breathtaking view a visitor has of Durham is the massive yet graceful outline of its cathedral. Even a rail traveller is favoured by two glimpses of the cathedral as the north or south-bound train winds its way high above the ancient city; once on the approach into the station and again as it leaves. Houses in the oldest part of Durham seem to huddle close to each other for mutual protection, apparently unable to believe that the threat of attack from Viking raiders, or Border reivers has long gone. Here was the home of the warlike Prince Bishops who controlled much of the North. The oldest part of the city fills the high promontory crowned by the cathedral, still retaining its medieval atmosphere, and where secret narrow alleys called 'vennels' offered an escape route to the river. This rocky promontory, being almost completely surrounded by a tight loop of the River Wear, has helped the oldest part of Durham to remain aloof from its modern suburbs.

The best way of exploring Durham is on foot, starting at its oldest and finest building — the **cathedral.** Approaching from Palace

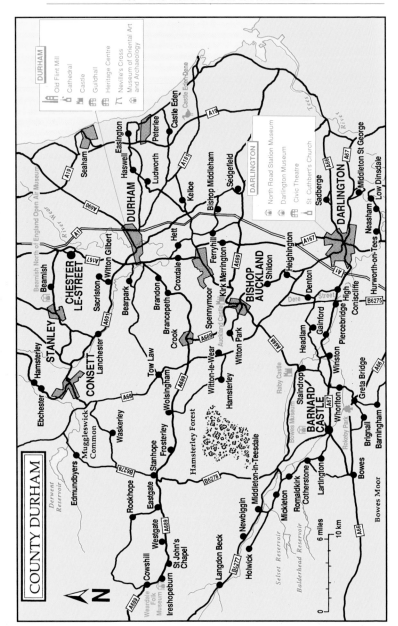

Durham Cathedral above the River Wear →

Green, the most striking feature on the massive main door is a monster's head which serves as a sanctuary knocker. Although only a replica (the original is in the cathedral's Treasury Museum), it is a faithful copy, including a hole made by a Scottish arrow. On entering the cathedral, the first impression that greets a visitor is the massive strength embodied in the Romanesque pillars supporting the nave roof. At the west end, to the right beyond the font, a line of Frosterley marble from Weardale is the demarkation beyond which women were forbidden to pass. At that time they had to worship in the Galilee Chapel, built in 1175 and now the resting place of the Venerable Bede. In the south transept is an astronomical clock from about 1500, which only displays 48 minutes. Moving into the main body of the cathedral, behind the high altar is the delicately beautiful Neville Screen, carved in 1375 from stone brought to Durham from Caen in Northern France. It acts as a backing for the cathedral's most important feature, the simple tomb of St Cuthbert who has rested there since 1104. Relics of the saint, including fragments of his coffin, his maniple (part of his vestments) and cross are on display in the Treasury Museum together with other precious items belonging to the cathedral's long history. The Chapel of the Nine Altars fills the east transept; built in the Early English style, it dates from 1242. Monks have not lived in the cathedral since the Dissolution in the sixteenth century. Their dormitory, dating from 1400, is now the library where many rare books and ancient manuscripts are kept. Elegant private houses line a quiet close behind the cathedral, together with an eighteenth-century water tower and the well-kept memorial garden to the seventh Durham Light Infantry.

Cobbled ways lead past the alms houses to **Durham Castle.** Begun as a palisaded motte and bailey mound, it was frequently attacked by the Scots even as late as the seventeenth century, when it was held for the Crown during the Civil War. It later became the official residence of incumbent Bishops of Durham until they moved to Aukland Palace and the castle became University College. The castle is open to visitors during the summer.

Georgian buildings lining North Bailey lead down to the Market Place where the fourteenth-century **Guildhall** has been incorporated within a Victorian town hall. Downhill to the right of the Market Place several fine medieval buildings surround twelfth-century Elvet Bridge, and further along in Hallgarth Street, a medieval tithe barn has stood the test of time.

Pleasant woodland footpaths follow the tightly curving River Wear below the cathedral and all are well away from traffic. Pedestrian bridges link both banks at Kingsgate Bridge, Framwellgate

Bridge, Prebends Bridge and Elvet Bridge. An alternative way to see the city and surrounding countryside is from a launch or rowing boat along the river. The landing stages are near Elvet Bridge.

The finest views of the cathedral are from the river near the corn mill opposite the fulling mill, or from Prebends Bridge below South Bailey. Floodlighting at night picks out the intricacies of the stonework and delicate pinnacles surmounting the towers and roof. As can be expected in an ecclesiastical city there are many ancient churches tucked away, often in hidden places and down side streets. St Nicholas is on Claypath, St Mary of Antioch in Crossgate. St Mary le Bow is where the body of St Cuthbert rested while the cathedral was being built. Durham has a wide range of museums: the Cathedral Treasury; Durham University's Museum of Oriental Art and Archaeology on Elvet Hill; the Heritage Centre in St Mary le Bow with its audio displays of Durham and the surrounding area; the Old Fulling Mill on the riverbank which illustrates the history of Durham; and the Durham Light Infantry Museum at Aykley Heads.

Neville's Cross is to the west of the city; it commemorates a decisive border battle fought close by in 1346, when the Scottish army led by King David II was beaten by the mixed forces of the Archbishop of York together with followers of the Percys and Nevilles.

Durham is the venue for the annual Durham Miners' Gala, an event that has a happy mix of politics and all-the-fun-of-the-fair. The political history of the Durham coalfield is graphically told on a mural to the right of and a little below the Market Place. Durham Regatta takes place every year on the broad waters of the Wear to the north of the city centre and is the oldest of its kind in Britain.

Mining villages, many with unusual sounding names, surround Durham. **Pity Me** on the Old North Road (A167), is perhaps the name that most fascinates visitors. The village is simply rows of miners' cottages built in the 1930s; the name is thought to be a corruption of *Petit Mere* — a little lake or pond — but this has since disappeared.

A side road from Pity Me, skirting the estates of Framwell Moor leads down towards the Wear, where the peaceful woodland setting of **Finchdale Priory**, a thirteenth-century Benedictine priory erected on the site of St Godric's hermitage, still merits the decision of its founders to build it there. The attractive site was used as a holiday retreat by monks from Durham Cathedral and although abandoned during the Dissolution, considerable remains of the church and claustral buildings have survived. There is a caravan and campsite and the riverbank is a popular picnic spot.

The Killhope Wheel Lead Mining Centre

Weardale

Once a heavily industrialised valley where lead ore and ironstone were mined beneath wild and often inhospitable moors, Weardale, in its upper reaches, has reverted to a tranquil rural dale where, with the abandoning of its earlier industry, time has stood still. One-time miners' cottages are now attractive homes for workers lower down the dale and one of the places which once employed hundreds of lead miners has been converted into a fascinating visitor centre. The River Wear rises near Killhope Cross on the border of County Durham and Northumberland, and the A689 from Alston climbs out of Nenthead to the county boundary before descending steeply, following the river into Weardale. Almost surrounded by plantations of mature pines, the **Killhope Wheel Lead Mining Centre**, once derelict, but now almost fully restored, is a fascinating insight into the life of the lead miner and the various stages of processing lead ore. The main and most striking feature of the complex is a giant overshot waterwheel, which powered the ore-crushing machinery. Other restored buildings include the working smithy, which is able to provide shoes for the sturdy Dales pony used in demonstrations of the old methods of transporting lead ore from mines high on the surrounding fells. A miners' 'shop', the cramped bunkhouse where they lived during their working week, often sleeping three and four to a bed, is laid out as part of a small but interesting museum with working displays and memorabilia of the region. There is a picnic site attached to the car park and many of the paths through the complex are accessible by wheelchair.

Ireshopeburn has two entirely different establishments to attract the visitor's attention: the Rancho del Rio, a converted farmhouse offering western-style entertainment; and near by, High House Chapel, which has been converted into the Weardale Museum, devoted to local customs and to lead mining. Built in 1760, the chapel has strong links with John Wesley who regularly preached in the area — at first beneath a hawthorn tree a short distance from the village. A commemorative plaque now identifies this tree and quotes 1749 as the date of his first visit.

Burnhope Reservoir to the west is pleasantly surrounded by a small plantation of pine trees; it can be reached by a short $1^3/_4$ mile footpath from Ireshopeburn, or along a quiet moorland road that rejoins the valley road at Cowshill.

Tiny hamlets and scattered farmsteads line the A689; most are at least a couple of centuries old, but Westernhopeburn (NY936379) is the least altered farmhouse in Weardale. Dated 1601, it is one continuous low stone structure in the medieval style, built to house family and animals under one roof. The road runs for a mile along the north side of the valley to reach **Westgate**, the western 'gate' of the Bishop of Durham's sixteenth-century deerpark. A cluster of stone cottages — one with a prominent clock — line the winding side street leading across the moor into Rookhope Dale. **Eastgate**, 4 miles on down the dale, sits below Weardale's rolling heather moors. At this point the dale is dominated by the chimney of a cement works; its hillside quarry is partly screened to the south, but nothing seems to escape the ever present dust.

There is an attractive waterfall in Rookhope Dale known as Low Linn, which can be reached by a short riverside footpath from Eastgate. A narrow road climbs Rookhope Dale, dividing about a mile beyond **Rookhope** with side roads going over the moors, north to Blanchland, south to Westgate and north-east out of the dale head to Allendale. It is hard to imagine that the straggling village of Rookhope was once the important industrial centre of a large lead and ironstone mining area. A railway once carried ironstone high across Stanhope moors, but it is now a mere cinder track, barely recognisable in places. In its day it was the highest standard gauge line in Britain. West of the B6278 Stanhope to Edmundbyers road, the railway is used as the **Waskerley Way** cycle track, footway and bridle track, and connects to the Derwent Walk Country Park beyond Consett.

The little town of **Stanhope** marks the boundary between pastoral Weardale and the wild heather moors to the west. Founded on lead mining and quarrying, Stanhope is now an important market town for the surrounding dales and farms, and the administrative centre for Upper Weardale. The oldest part of the town sits back from an irregular-shaped square, with its ancient market cross. The western end of the square ends abruptly with a rather incongruous view of the rear of battlemented Stanhope Castle. Its unattractive appearance from the main street contrasts with its more striking aspect from the river. The house has had a chequered career; built in 1747 and once a school, it has now been converted into flats. There is a far more interesting building across the road from the castle; the parish church of St Thomas dates mainly from the thirteenth century and contains a Roman altar dedicated to Silvanus, the woodland god. The altar was found on Bollihope Common, a source of many ancient relics, in 1747. The church has several pieces of medieval stained glass in its windows, but the strangest feature of all is the fossilized tree stump in the graveyard wall which was found beneath the moors above Edmundbyers. Seventeenth-century Stanhope Old Hall is to the west of the town. Its solid bulk has the appearance of an old mill, probably because some of the older windows were filled in during the days when a window tax was levied on properties. Down a side road, past the swimming pool and across a pretty ford to the south of the town, is the strangely named Unthank Hall. An Elizabethan manor house, its name (from an Old English word meaning 'without leave') indicates that it was held by squatters at one time. Westwards from the hall and following the river upstream a fifteenth-century bridge that carries the road to Teesdale, the B6278 across a narrow gorge, where after heavy rain the water level can rise with alarming rapidity.

Just over 2 miles down the dale is **Frosterley**, a straggle of terraced cottages, mostly the homes of quarrymen whose grandfathers dug the famous Frosterley black marble. This unique marble is in fact a limestone speckled by countless fossils, and is still in demand for its decorative beauty, although not in the quantities of Victorian times. Frosterley is built on ancient foundations and is even mentioned in the *Boldon Beuk*, the 1183 equivalent of the Domesday Book. Although no buildings survive from that time, a bridge hundreds of years old crosses the Wear to the west of the village carrying the once important road south into Teesdale.

Industry in central Weardale, other than mining or quarrying, can be said to begin at **Wolsingham**, a mixture of old stone cottages and modern developments in a rural setting. There are one or two houses are of special note; namely the eighteenth-century Whitfield House, a three-storied town house with an almost French provincial air and next to it is Whitfield Place, a seventeenth-century building with attractive mullioned windows. The church tower is twelfth-century, but the main body of the church is mid-Victorian in the Early English style. Wolsingham holds an annual show during the first weekend in September, which is quite an ambitious affair for such a small town.

Both brown and migratory trout inhabit the Wear, as well as the occasional salmon. Tunstall Reservoir, 2 miles to the north, is stocked with brown and rainbow trout. Rod licences and day permits can be bought locally. To the south, Hamsterley Forest fills most of Bedburn Burn valley. There is a Forest Drive (toll), and walks and picnic sites.

Hamsterley, the village that gives its name to the forest, and not to be confused with its namesake in the Derwent Valley north of Consett, sits on a broad ridge between Bedburn and Linburn Becks. Its church is Early English and a mile north-west is the nineteenth-century Bedburn Mill, a watermill of considerable architectural and archaeological merit, which is currently being restored. To the north of the mill, about a mile along the Wolsingham road, a lodge looking like something out of a fairy tale once guarded the drive to Hoppyland Hall. Only the mellow ruins of this eighteenth-century house remain, and its parkland has reverted to nature, where the naturalized rhododendrons are a blaze of colour in late spring. Just over a mile north of Hamsterley, and above Harthope Beck, The Castles is a large enigmatic mound, ancient but of uncertain date, surrounded by a wooded moat.

The Wear makes a bend to the south-east below Wolsingham, before turning northwards and meandering through the increasingly industrial countryside of the Durham plain. The countryside south-east of Witton-le-Wear is a charming hotch-potch of agricultural and one-time mining villages with evocative names like Butterknowle and Evenwood. **Witton-le-Wear** is a village of great character and antiquity built around a narrow green on a south-facing slope above the river. A peel tower, part of a medieval manor house, is at the upper end of the village and dates from less peaceful times. The church is thirteenth century, but was rebuilt early this century. Witton Castle, across the Wear from the village, is a curious mixture of styles and additions built around the original fourteenth-century keep. There is a camping and caravan site within the grounds. Witton Park, to the south-east, is an industrial hamlet built around a now abandoned coal mine. Floodplains and woodlands between the two Wittons have been designated as a nature reserve, haunt of both woodland birds and waterfowl.

A side road leaves the Witton-le-Wear road to reach **Escomb**. The road leads past modern houses and farms to Escomb's main attraction, one of the finest and least altered Saxon churches in England. Probably built during the Venerable Bede's lifetime, it features stones plundered from *Vinovia*, the Roman fort at Binchester. One of them is inscribed *Leg VI*, indicating the sixth Legion, which was based there. The construction of the church is typical of its time, with a tall narrow nave and chancel, any additions being confined to two or three of the larger windows. Parts of the original cobbled floor are intact and the sundial is still in position, the oldest of its kind in England. Escomb owes its happy preservation to being neglected by the Victorians who, despite their zeal for 'improving' churches, abandoned this one in favour of a new one higher up the hill. The wheel of fortune has gone full circle — the Victorian church has been demolished, the Saxon one carefully restored to its former glory. Escomb's houses, old as well as new in the centre of the village, sit in roughly concentric circles around the church, filling the sites where the houses of the original Saxon village stood.

Bishop Auckland, an industrial town with a dignified heart built on ancient foundations, marks the north-eastern bend of the Wear. Bishops of Durham have used Auckland Castle and its surrounding deerpark since the twelfth century. The castle is to the north-east of the centre of the older and finest part of the town, and is approached through an imposing gateway. Originally a Norman manor house, it was largely rebuilt in 1760. Within are splendid state rooms with delicate tracery in their plaster ceilings. Bishop Cosin designed much of the magnificent woodwork and panelling in the chapel of St Peter, a building of breathtaking yet delicate proportions, much larger than one would expect for a private chapel. It was in fact a banqueting hall before its conversion by Bishop Cosin. Beyond the castle and across a shallow valley is the Deercote or Sanctuary, an open stone square structure with viewing towers (now closed) set in 800 acres of parkland and woods. The park and deer sanctuary are open to the public, but Auckland Castle, the official residence, is private, and only the chapel and state rooms are open, from May to September.

The town has had a market since medieval times and elegant buildings on either side of the old market square indicate a prosperity which continued throughout later centuries. Bishop Auckland grew from a scattered group of hamlets between the steep south bank of the River Wear and its tributary the Gaunless. The parish church of St Andrew is Saxon in origin. Said to be the largest church in County Durham, its greatest feature is a Saxon cross reconstructed from fragments found during rebuilding work in 1881.

The Wear is spanned by a fifteenth-century bridge below the town and also a nineteenth-century viaduct. The latter is now used as a footpath, part of the $9^1/_2$ mile Bishop Brandon Walk from Bishop Auckland to Broompark picnic site on the outskirts of Durham.

Roman Dere Street passed north-westwards through what became Bishop Auckland from York to Corbridge. A little to the north of the town along a minor road following a sweeping bend of the Wear is Binchester, site of the Roman fort of *Vinovia*, which means 'pleasant spot'. The name probably refers to the excellent views of the river which are now enhanced by Auckland Castle. The partially excavated remains are in the care of Durham County Council, and the most readily appreciated outlines are those of the hypocaust, a Roman central heating system. Nineteenth-century Binchester Hall is to one side of the fort; until fairly recently it was an hotel, but its future is now in doubt.

The last part of this section devoted to Weardale describes places to the west of the A1(M) and south of the Wear, before moving north of the river to investigate those towns and villages which lie between Durham City and Tyneside. Finally, the guide moves east from the motorway and out towards the coast.

South of the Wear and West of the A1(M)

The A6072 leaves the south-eastern outskirts of Bishop Auckland and crosses the Gaunless to reach **Shildon**, a town which grew with the fortunes of the Durham coalfield. George Stephenson was invited to build a track from Witton Park, via Shildon and Darlington, to the harbour facilities at Stockton-on-Tees. Originally intended to move only coal, the line was so successful that following the demands of the local population, fare-paying passengers began to be carried, beginning their journey from near Timothy Hackworth's home in Shildon. Hackworth was one of the lesser-known founding fathers of the railway system. He built the *Sans Pareil*, one of the first engines to be made, which pre-dated Stephenson's more famous *Locomotion Number One*. His home, in the centre of Shildon, is now a museum and is linked by the Surtees Trail to many of the still-recognizable features of the original railway. The trail runs from Hackworth's Soho Engine Works to Daniel Adam's Coach House, the Shildon terminus of a second branch of the Stockton and Darlington Railway. A working replica of *Sans Pareil* stands outside the Soho Works paint shop. Further relics of the birth of the railway age can be found along an unclassified road to the west linking Shildon with the A68. These are the stone sleepers on the Brusselton Incline, an important section of the original route of the Stockton and Darlington Railway.

Moving north, **Croxdale**, a cluster of miners' cottages, is built around the junction of the A167 and B6288 (Spennymoor road). The main features here are the dramatic bridges crossing the deep cleft made by the Wear. Sunderland Bridge is thirteenth-century and lies below a modern road bridge; then upstream a railway viaduct carries the London-Edinburgh main railway line towards Durham. Croxdale Hall and its famous orangery is across the railway line. Burn Hall sits above a bend of the River Browney prior to its confluence with the Wear and to the west of the A167.

North of the Wear and West of the A1(M)

To explore this part of County Durham, follow the Wear's north bank upstream as far as the A68 before turning north, and using Durham City as a pivot, cross the tributary valleys of the Deerness and Browney, then on reaching the Tyne flowing Derwent valley, turn east towards the coast.

Following the A690 south-west from Durham, the first place of note is **Brancepeth**. This attractive Victorian estate village is dominated by the massive strength of its castle and its 'chess-men' watchtowers. The castle's origins go back to Saxon times, but much of the present building dates from the nineteenth century and is split up into private dwellings. The village post office is a gem, and fits smugly into one of the gate-house towers.

The adjacent church of St Brandon is old, mostly thirteenth century, but its main attractions are the seventeenth-century interior panelling and carved ceiling, a double-decker pulpit and the splendidly carved chancel screen.

On through Willington to the spacious little town of **Crook**. The town's central feature is a wide square surrounded by pleasant greens and flower beds. Quaintly named Billy Row to the north of the town centre is a typical Durham coalfield hamlet of miner's cottages. A little further north, across the B6299 and down a side road from Stanley Crook, is the start of the Deerness Valley walk, a linear footpath mostly using an abandoned railway track as far as Neville's Cross on the outskirts of Durham.

By turning north along the A68, **Tow Law** is soon reached, a former mining community at the junction of five roads on a bleak hilltop in a rural setting. Tow Law's church is worth visiting if only to see the delightfully artistic screen made of fir cones, acorns, walnuts and chestnuts.

Turning right to join the B6301, the road links a series of small towns and villages above the Deerness Valley, all interconnected by a cat's cradle of minor roads. The valley towns of Esh Winning, Bearpark and Ushaw Moor are expanding suburbs of Durham based on ex-mining villages. The tiny hilltop village of **Esh** is not to be confused with its larger neighbour Esh Winning. The unusually sounding name is from the Old English for 'ash tree'. Its parish church, though much restored, still bears traces of its Saxon foundations. An ancient cross on the village green marks the spot where St Cuthbert's body rested during its long journey around Northumbria. The hall is seventeenth century, but only traces of this once great building are left, incorporated within the farmhouse on its site.

About three quarters of a mile to the west of Bearpark (the name incidentally has nothing to do with bears, but is a corruption of *beau repaire*: it was the country seat of Durham priors in the Middle Ages), **Ushaw College** stands square on the skyline. This famous Roman Catholic seminary was founded by Bishop Allen in 1568, and was originally based at Douai in Northern France. After several moves the present site was chosen in 1808. The college still retains many of the traditions established at Douai, including its own form of squash: the Douai game, as it is known. Ushaw is open to visitors by prior arrangement.

Crossing the River Browney to reach the A691, where **Witton Gilbert** (the 'G' is pronounced soft as in 'ginger'), developed as a mining community in the nineteenth century, but has earlier foundations. The church has a unique double bell tower and was rebuilt in 1863. Even so, it retains many links with its Norman origins, especially on the south side of the nave and in the chancel. The hall was once a leper hospital, traces of which still remain, including a thirteenth-century window. A mile or so west along the main road, and in dense woodland, lie the sad ruins of Langley Hall. This was once a sixteenth-century courtyard house built by Lord Scrope of Bolton, but was abandoned in the eighteenth century.

Continuing north-west along the A691, the road passes through **Lanchester**, a small town which spreads itself comfortably around a wide green, mostly beyond a side stream feeding the Browney. Everything is dominated by the tall, embattlemented tower of its Norman and Early English church, a building of considerable architectural and archaeological interest. Of particular note are the number of Roman altarstones and pillars from the nearby fort that are incorporated into the building.

The Romans built their fort of *Longovicium* near modern Lanchester, on Dere Street, their road linking York and Hadrian's Wall. Little of the fort, which is at the side of the B6296 on the outskirts of the town, is visible, for most of its above-ground stones were later plundered for building material. However, several of its altars were saved, and are in Durham Cathedral as well as the local church.

Fires from **Consett**'s furnaces no longer light the night sky and dull the daylight with their belching smoke and steam. Nothing remains of a steelworks that once stretched for over a mile across the broad ridge. Consett developed as a tight-knit community, and it is this community spirit that is helping the town recover from the almost mortal blow of losing its livelihood in such a dramatic manner.

The Derwent Walk Country Park, using a redundant railway line north of the town, follows the Derwent Valley, and to the south, the Waskerley Way is based on an abandoned ironstone railway on to the moors above Weardale.

The Derwent forms part of the north-eastern boundary between County Durham and Northumberland. Dere Street, the Roman road, crossed the river immediately to the north of Consett, a crossing the Romans guarded with their fort of *Vindomora*. The village of **Ebchester** now occupies the same position. The village church is built into the fort's south-west corner. It is basically Norman, but was very much altered in the nineteenth century and has many Roman stones in its fabric.

About $1^1/_2$ miles downstream along the A694, **Hamsterley** (there is another village of the same name in Weardale), was the home of the celebrated nineteenth-century novelist Robert Surtees, creator of Jorrocks, the sporting grocer. Surtees lived at Hamsterley Hall to the east of the village.

Upsteam is the Derwent Reservoir, planned for its amenity value as well as for storing water. Sailing, fishing, picnic sites and bird watching are all catered for on and around this now naturalized feature. Pow Hill Country Park has been established along the southern shore. A little to the south of the reservoir, **Edmundbyers** lies at the foot of the heather moors of Muggleswick Common. It once had two pubs, but the oldest is now a youth hostel. The church was founded in 1150 and has the remains of a witch, once common in the district, buried in its graveyard. As though warding off their evil influence, a single eye decorates the squint of its circular west window. **Waskerley** (NY052454), high to the south on Muggleswick Common, is probably the most isolated hamlet in County Durham. It owes its existence to the high-level railway line which once ran

A reconstructed town centre at the Beamish Open Air Museum

from Weardale to Consett and provided homes for workers on the line. An incline ran from Waskerley to Rowley on the A68, and it is possible to trace the route of this now abandoned line by using the Waskerley Way long distance footpath.

A signpost off the A693 points the way to the **Beamish North of** **England Open Air Museum**, a re-creation of northern life as it was around the turn of the century. The minor road leads past the Shepherd and Shepherdess, a Georgian public house with two romantically styled figures for its inn sign. Entering beneath the massive frame of a forge hammer, the visitor can climb aboard a 1930s tramcar to reach the various sections of the museum. Farm machinery, heavy industrial plant, steam operated fairground rides and replica early locomotives mostly in full working order, are on display in the open air. Pride of place is the 1920s Town Street, a collection of furnished houses, including a dentist's surgery and solicitor's office, print shop, a working pub and the fully stocked co-operative shop, moved lock, stock and barrel from Annfield Plain. There is a small Edwardian park with a band stand and on the far side of the complex. Home Farm has a collection of old farm implements, some of them steam driven, and unusual breeds of animals. Beyond is the colliery area with its row of single-storied miners' cottages, each furnished to show the changing styles of furniture throughout the last century. Visitors can go underground into a drift mine on a small colliery train. Rowley Station taken from the Waskerley line, re-creates the atmosphere of steam railways. Not surprisingly, Beamish was given the accolade of Museum of the Year in 1987.

Beamish Hall is across a minor road at the side of the main part of the museum and houses an amazing collection of objects ranging from miners' lamps, to handmade Durham quilts. Footpaths link the Beamish museum with the single span of Causey Arch about a mile to the north, at the side of the A6076 (NZ205560). Built in 1727 to carry horse-drawn railway wagons from a local colliery, it is considered to be the oldest railway bridge in the world.

The bustling part market, part industrial town, of **Chester-le-Street** is crammed around the confluence of Cow Burn and the River Wear, restricted from eastward development by the A167 trunk road and the A1 motorway. The main line to the north crosses the town centre by a massive viaduct. Chester's 'Street' is a Roman road later followed by the Great North Road, now the A6127, from Binchester to *Pons Aelius* or modern Newcastle upon Tyne. The town's roots reach back to the *vicus* or civilian settlement that developed in the protection of a Roman fort.

The church, first built to hold the coffin of St Cuthbert and rebuilt in the eleventh century, was later rebuilt in the thirteenth century. Further restoration work was carried out in Victorian and more recent times. The spire dates from around 1400 and is considered to be the finest in County Durham.

Pride of place in modern Chester-le-Street is the civic centre. The all-glass, open plan municipal office is readily accessible to the public, in an attempt to make local government less intimidating. Indoor trees and a restaurant all add to the informal nature of this courageous experiment.

Several fine Georgian and Victorian town houses stand out amid the modern developments. Once the homes of rich coal owners, the most notable are the Hermitage, a mock Tudor manor house to the south of the town; and Southill Hall a fine late-Georgian house, standing in its own well-wooded grounds. Waldridge Fell Country Park is about a mile along a minor road south-west of the town County Durham's last surviving lowland heath. Access is open to the whole of its 300 acres by waymarked footpaths. **Lumley Castle** lies to the east of the town on the opposite side of the Wear. Now a hotel with a golf course, the castle is set in elevated parkland and dates from the fourteenth century. A popular venue for medieval banquets, it even has its own ghostly white lady, the Lily of Lumley!

East of the A1 Motorway

Tiny villages are hidden well away from busy arterial roads connecting the new towns of County Durham's coastal plain. Their churches give some indication of their age, but some are built on foundations older even than Christianity. Industry and under-sea collieries tend to dominate much of the coastline, but many of the denes — short, deep-cut, wooded valleys, a feature of this part of the north-east coast — run down to attractive little sandy beaches.

Seaham, or Seaham Harbour as it is more usually known, developed as a port in the nineteenth century to ship Durham coal to its widespread markets. The church of St Mary the Virgin is over 900 years old and is in the oldest part of the town. Seaham Hall, on the northern outskirts, is now a hospital. The hall has links with the poet Byron, for it was here that he met and married Isabella Millbanke in 1815. Seaham has a number of pleasantly laid-out parks and open spaces, as well as long stretches of firm sandy beaches. Sea angling is a popular sport in the area, both from inshore boats, or beach casting. There is an annual 'All Comers' competition each autumn.

The motorist's view of **Easington**, driving south along the A19, is of a pleasant group of houses around a thirteenth-century church, proof that colliery villages can look attractive. The village is divided between Easington proper and Easington Colliery where, in 1951 eighty men were killed in the worst mining disaster in modern times. The accident is commemorated by a brilliantly coloured and gilded screen and altar, specially commissioned for the red-brick Church of the Ascension in the colliery village. For a long time Easington was represented by the eminent Labour polititian, the late Emanuel Shinwell, who became Lord Shinwell.

The crumbling ruin of thirteenth-century Seaton Holme in the centre of Easington village is supposed to be built on the site of an eleventh-century house once owned by Nicholas Breakspear. He became Adrian IV (died 1159), the only English pope. Over to the west along a side road, a ruined tower at **Haswell** which looks as though it could be Roman, is in fact an abandoned colliery winding tower. It was built as a folly and is the sole link with the now-defunct industry of the village. There is another ruined tower a couple of miles to the south-west at **Ludworth**, all that is left of a once great manor house built by Sir Thomas Holden in 1422.

A side road off the A19 leads to **Peterlee**, a new town created in 1948 and named after Peter Lee, chairman of the first Labour controlled Durham County Council. A couple of miles inland from the sea, the town is built across gently rolling countryside, a feature which has been used to full advantage by its developers. Castle Eden

Dene, a deep-cut wooded ravine created by glacial melt-water, is to the south of Peterlee. It is now a nature reserve, but was romantically landscaped by Rowland Burdon at the end of the eighteenth century. Footpaths lead down from both sides of the valley and there is an interpretive centre at Oakerside Dene Lodge. Over seventy species of birds and many rare moths and butterflies have been identified throughout the site.

The village of **Castle Eden** takes its name from the three-storied eighteenth-century castle. At one time the castle was the regional headquarters of the National Coal Board, but it now belongs to Peterlee Corporation; there is a golf course in the park. The neat little village has its own real-ale brewery which is housed in a white-washed cupola-topped group of buildings, used as a cotton mill in the eighteenth century. The church is ancient, but was rebuilt in 1764 by Rowland Burdon after he found it in ruinous decay, according to a plaque above the vestry door.

South of Castle Eden village another wooded valley, Crimdon Beck, has a caravan site above its sandy beach. The dene also marks the boundary between County Durham and Cleveland.

Kelloe is in the middle of countryside marred by quarrying, but its antecedents go back as far as the Bronze Age. Traces of a large settlement have been found to the south near Garmondsway Farm (NZ342348). King Canute is supposed to have made a barefoot pilgrimage from Kelloe to Durham in 1017 to visit the shrine of St Cuthbert. The modern village is mostly miners' cottages and council estates, but the heavily buttressed church is Norman. Its greatest relic is the Kelloe Cross which depicts St Helena's vision of the Holy Cross as well as showing other versions of the saint together with an unknown companion. She is also shown menacing Judas Iscariot, ordering him to dig with a spade and discover the cross.

Elizabeth Barrett Browning was born at nearby Coxhoe Hall (demolished in the 1950s) in 1806. She was baptized in Kelloe church, an event commemorated by a monument erected by public sub-scription in 1897. Another less happy monument is to the memory of seventy-four miners who were killed in a mining disaster at Trimdon Pit in 1822.

All through-roads, the A689, A177 and even the B1278, manage to skirt **Sedgefield**, a pleasant market town set in lush open country and where the modern houses manage to blend well with its pantiled cottages. Thirteenth-century St Edmund's Church, an impressive example of the Early English style, overlooks the town centre. Sedgefield is one of the few towns in England to hold a traditional Shrove Tuesday football match, a game far removed from the

Memorial fountain
Middleton-in-Teesdale

modern game. A town walk exploring the interesting byways and old buildings, is described in the Durham County Council's *Walkabout Booklet No 7: Sedgefield*. There is a racecourse across the A689 to the south-west of the town, and opposite it is Hardwick Hall, a sixteenth-century house with a fine eighteenth-century front. The park with a lake covering 36 acres, a temple of Minerva, as well as follies and a grotto, are all that is left of a grandiose scheme which ran out of money before it was finished. Hardwick, with its bog nature trail, is now a country park in the care of Durham County Council.

Teesdale

The Tees rises less than 200ft below the summit of Cross Fell, the highest point on the Pennines, and for much of its early life flows through the North Pennines Area of Outstanding Natural Beauty. In its upper reaches, the wild moors have been specially designated as a National Nature Reserve where plants more commonly found in sub-arctic regions can be found. It was this special character which led to an outcry from environmentalists when the proposal was made to create **Cow Green Reservoir**. Access to the reservoir is by a 3 mile drive along a minor road west across Widdybank Fell from the lonely moorland farming community of **Langdon Beck**. The dramatic setting of this stretch of water backed by Cross Fell and its satellites, partly absolves the vandalism of drowning such an environmentally sensitive area. A waymarked nature trail from the car park passes sites where rare subalpine plants such as the spring gentian (*Gentiana Verna*) grow. Below the dam wall, the released river surges over outcropping dolerite in the splendid cataract of **Cauldron Snout**. There is a rough footpath extending from the Nature Trail and it is necessary to follow it to admire the full spectacle of the falls, but it can be slippery at times. The Pennine Way long distance footpath links Langdon Beck in upper Teesdale with Dufton at the western foot of Cross Fell, the only places where accommodation can be found on this particularly wild remote section of the arduous walk. Whitewashed farmhouses and cottages dotting the fellsides of this part of upper Teesdale, are part of the Raby Estate.

About 6 miles down the valley, the turbulent river reaches High Force, the highest above-ground waterfall and certainly one of the most attractive, in England. A short footpath through the grounds of High Force Hotel, where a small toll must be paid, leads down to the riverbank a few yards downstream from the falls. Low Force, more a series of rapids over low rocky outcrops, is further downstream; less dramatic than High Force, it is equally as attractive in a delightful sylvan setting near Bowlees. 'Force' derives from the Old Norse word 'foss', meaning a waterfall.

Low Force marks the beginning of the gentler part of the Tees. A scattering of roadside cottages alongside the B6277 are indicated by the wayside sign **Newbiggin**. The village was once an important lead mining centre with its own smelter; the name Newbiggin, common in Northern England, is Old Norse in origin and means 'new building', or 'house'. The valley chapel at **Bowlees** has been converted into a visitor centre which explains the natural history of Upper Teesdale in an easy-to-follow, yet well documented manner. A related nature trail to Gibson's Cave starts from the centre and leads through about half a mile of woodland, to a small cave hollowed out of the shaley rock by an attractive little waterfall.

From Newbiggin a field path leads down to Scoberry Bridge; across the Tees a riverside path follows the bank upstream to the rapids of Low Force. Wynch Bridge close by can be used to regain the opposite bank, where more field paths lead back to Newbiggin, making a very pleasant $2^1/_2$ mile walk. Wynch Bridge is built on the site of the first suspension bridge in Europe: the original was put up in 1744 to give access to nearby lead mines.

Across the valley from Newbiggin and reached either by a 4 mile 'no through road' north-west from Middleton-in-Teesdale, or by footpaths above both Scoberry and Wynch bridges, **Holwick**, a tiny group of farms, cottages and a pub, fits snugly beneath the crags of Holwick Scars. A short walk of less than half a mile through Mill Beck Wood, to the east of Holwick, leads to an attractive waterfall. Known as Fairy Dell, it is on private land, but permission is usually granted to anyone wishing to picnic or ramble there: enquire at the Strathmore Arms in Holwick.

Middleton-in-Teesdale, the 'capital' of upper Teesdale, grew in the nineteenth-century when it became the headquarters of the London Lead Company. Its most striking feature is its wide, grassy main street with the elaborate cast-iron Bainbridge drinking fountain at one end. Cattle auctions, quaint shops and one-time coaching inns complete the rural scene. The church is Victorian, but replaced an earlier, probably Norman, foundation. Stotley Hall is about $1^1/_2$ miles to the east, along the Barnard Castle road, a fine and attractive example of a prosperous seventeenth-century farmhouse.

The linear village of **Mickleton** is across the Tees and is where Neolithic burial sites have been found on the nearby fells. The B6276 climbs past the enigmatic and prominent clump of trees known as Kirkcarrion to climb Lunedale and cross bleak Stainmore Common to Brough, a town built on the site of a Roman fort which guarded the east-west crossing of the Pennines. The route of this Roman road is now followed by the A66(T), Scotch Corner to Penrith road.

Two reservoirs impound the waters of the Lune; the Upper, Selset, has been made available to anglers and members of a sailing club, while the lower reservoir, long and narrow Grassholme, is the preserve of anglers only. Day tickets to fish both waters, and those in Baldersdale immediately to the south, are available locally (see Further Information).

Romaldkirk stands at the junction of the B6277 and a narrow road which climbs to a dead end near the top of Baldersdale. One of the prettiest villages in Teesdale, it takes its name from Anglo-Saxon St Rumwald who built its first church. Set in a green and pleasant landscape above the River Tees and backed by rolling moorland to the south and west, the village is a delightfully haphazard grouping of stone-built cottages around a series of greens and narrow alleyways. The rectory is Georgian and the church a mixture of styles dating back at least to the twelfth century.

A castle once defended **Cotherstone** at the mouth of Baldersdale;

built in the twelfth century, only a few small mounds remain. The village, however, is a charming group of stone cottages and one or two larger houses on either side of the B6277 which follows the west side of the Tees between Barnard Castle and Middleton-in-Teesdale. The cosy village of **Lartington** is a little over a mile to the south of Cotherstone. Woodland shelters it from the north winds and the village is the home of estate workers at Lartington Hall. The annual Teesdale Country Fair takes place in Lartington Park.

Three reservoirs have been created in Baldersdale. Balderhead

Bowes Museum near Barnard Castle

and Hury have been stocked with trout and are available to anglers, but the middle one, Blackton is not. Pennine Way walkers greet their arrival in Baldersdale with something bordering relief, for this is exactly half-way along the arduous 270-mile trek. A footpath south-east over Cotherstone Moor passes below the curious gritstone cap known as Goldsborough, probably the most northerly site associated with the legendary hero Robin Hood.

Moving back to the east side of Teesdale, **Eggleston** marks the division between the wild northern moors and the lush lower reaches of the dale. Several ancient trading routes, including drove roads, came through Eggleston. A tangible link with those more leisurely forms of transport is the seventeenth-century packhorse bridge across the village stream. The church is Victorian, built to replace an earlier one, the ruins of which can be seen in the grounds of Eggleston Hall to the south of the main part of the village. The hall, a private residence, is a fine example of a Victorian country gentleman's house.

Administrative centre for Upper Teesdale, **Barnard Castle** marks the division between fell and plain, a bustling yet charming market town at the junction of seven roads which developed within the protection of a Norman castle. Built on a commanding height above the Tees, the castle commanded an important north-south river crossing, still marked by a bridge built in 1569, which can still cope with present-day traffic. Now maintained in immaculate condition by English Heritage, it is possible to gain an accurate impression of its original size from the surviving walls and neat lawns that were once the site of crude buildings and stables housing the castle's retainers and their animals.

Streets radiate from the castle with names like Bridgegate, Newgate and Thorngate. Stately eighteenth-century houses line Thorngate, which descends past an old watermill to an attractive footbridge giving access to riverside walks beside the Tees. On the right as you descend is a shop specialising in dolls' houses, both made-up and in kit form. Opposite is sixteenth-century Blagroves House, with gabled windows on three storeys, giving the appearance of a tall narrow tower butted on to the main building. A substantial octagonal market cross built in 1747 stands in the market place at the top of Thorngate. Crowned by a cupola and weathervane, the colonnaded shelter has been used by generations of local people selling farm produce. The town hall, lit by elegant Venetian windows, fills the upper storey. Barnard Castle's church is to the east of the cross; much altered in the nineteenth century, it is nevertheless built on Norman foundations.

Beyond the market place, the street becomes Horsemarket and on the left is the King's Head, where Charles Dickens stayed in 1838 when collecting material for his novel *Nicholas Nickleby*. In Newgate a plaque marks the site of a shop owned by the man who was the inspiration for another of Dicken's novels, *Master Humphries' Clock*, itself intended as the frame for both *Barnaby Rudge* and *The Old Curiosity Shop*.

A little to the east of the town centre, along Newgate from the market cross, is the Bowes Museum. The building was designed as a museum, not a residence, and Bowes laid the foundation stone in 1869, but both he and his French actress wife died before it was completed. In accordance with his wishes, the museum opened in 1892. Now run by the Durham County Council Museums Service, it is filled with objects ranging from locally found Roman relics to paintings by El Greco, Goya and other masters, as well as period furniture and fashions. Of all the many and varied exhibits, visitors usually retain a lasting impression of the silver lifesize working model of a swan which is given pride of place in the entrance hall. Not only does it appear to glide on water, but it actually catches small fishes! Check its time of operation and plan to be in the entrance hall at the appropriate time to witness a sight not to be missed. Formal parkland surrounds the museum which is open daily except Christmas and the New Year.

Stately homes and historic castles add character to the rural landscape surrounding Barnard Castle. A couple of miles north-east along the A688 Bishop Auckland road, **Streatlam Park** marks the site of where a castle and grand three-storeyed mansion once stood. The remaining features as seen from the road, are the elegant eighteenth-century gates and twin lodges built in Classical style, the original entrance to the park.

The main road runs through gently undulating pastureland to a complex junction of 'B' roads on either side of **Staindrop**, an attractive grouping of mellow stone houses on either side of a long village green, and home village for Raby Castle. The tall-towered church includes Norman and later elements; narrow, now blocked-off windows speak of its Saxon antecedents. The screen is pre-Reformation, the only one in County Durham. The Lords of Raby are buried here in splendid tombs. Staindrop House, a mellow sandstone building on the narrow street leading to the church, is mostly Jacobean.

Raby Castle is at the side of the Bishop Auckland road, a little under a mile to the north of Staindrop, and the road skirts the eastern boundary of the park. Deer and sheep wander freely in the 200 acres of landscaped park surrounding the medieval battlemented castle. Despite Victorian adaptations and modernising in the cause of creature comforts, the castle retains much of its earlier atmosphere. Many of the features are original, such as the 600-year-old great kitchen with its glowing collection of Victorian copper utensils. Long vaulted passageways evoke a time when the castle was bustling with activity. Crossing the beautiful parkland, the visitor enters the castle through its awesome fourteenth-century gatehouse guarded by warlike statues. Beyond the gate, Clifford's Tower dominates the

Egglestone Abbey

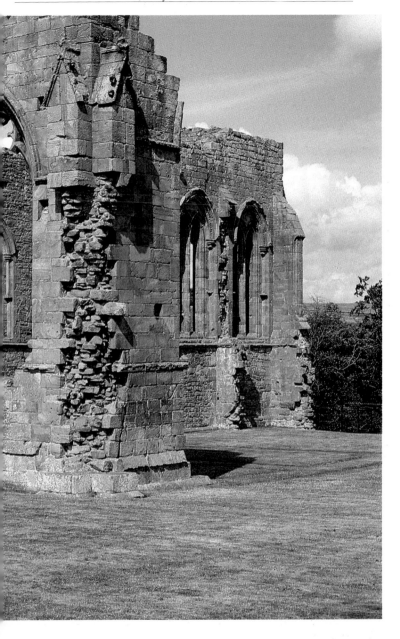

view, enough to strike terror into any attackers. Fortunately those days are long gone, and it is now possible to walk peacefully around the perimeter walls. There is a fine collection of horse drawn vehicles used by the Barnard family on display in the coach house, and outside the large walled gardens and ancient yew hedges are a further link with the past. The castle and gardens are usually open to the public from Easter to the end of September.

The River Greta flows roughly due east from Bowes Moor on Stainmore, a wilderness of boggy moorland crossed by the A66(T), a road still marked by the sites of Roman forts and signal stations. A drove road south from Teesdale into Swaledale once crossed the river by a natural limestone arch known as God's Bridge (NY957126). The 'bridge' is now used by walkers travelling north or south along the Pennine Way.

God's Bridge is linked to **Bowes** by $2^1/_2$ miles of riverside footpaths and farm lanes. The village marks the eastern end of the Stainmore crossing, a site first guarded by the Roman fort of *Lavatris*. Later, during the reign of Henry II, a Norman castle was built by William d'Arcubus to command this important east-west crossing of the Pennines. The massive walls of the keep are still standing amidst the grassy outline of the Roman fort; both are in the care of English Heritage.

Before the advent of motorised transport, horse-drawn coaches braving the crossing of Stainmore paused at the eighteenth-century Unicorn Inn, which still graces the quiet village street. Charles Dickens left the east-west mailcoach at the Unicorn when he was researching material for *Nicholas Nickleby*. The novel is based on a boy's academy in this remote village run by its owner, William Shaw. He became the sadistic Wackford Squeers in the story and the house alleged to be the model for Dotheboys Hall is at the western end of the village. Now that traffic speeding along the busy A66 safely bypasses the village, Bowes makes an ideal base to explore the footpaths and moors on either side of the Greta. There is a riverside caravan and campsite at Mellwaters Farm about 2 miles to the west of Bowes.

An unclassified side road leaves the A66 near Boldron to travel south into Arkengarthdale, a subsidiary of Swaledale. Just below Hope Edge, near the highest point of this road, Stang Forest has a couple of scenic car parks and a series of short Forest Walks. The same road also gains access to a deeply cut narrow wooded section of the Greta valley. Known as Brignall Banks, the valley has footpaths along both sides of its 4-mile course. The romantic ruin of St Mary's church is on the western bank of the river, over a quarter of a mile from **Brignall** village. The church once served the surrounding hamlets, but no doubt villagers became tired of the long damp walk, so in 1833 built one more convenient for themselves, although the old church continued to be used for burials for another 50 years.

South of the dale and almost on the border with North Yorkshire, **Barningham** marks the division between pasture and moor. It has a wide green lined by stone cottages in a charming grouping of styles and sizes. The church is Victorian Gothic with a graveyard of moss-covered tombstones. Barningham Park is late seventeenth century with the addition of an eighteenth-century stable block. The whole is set in attractive gardens and terraced woodland walks. A series of Roman shrines were discovered on Scargill Moor (NY995104) to the west of Barningham. Altarstones and details of the excavation are on display in Bowes Museum.

The A66 crosses the river at Greta Bridge and about half a mile to the north-west, a side road leading to Barnard Castle passes the entrance to **Rokeby Park**. The magnificent Palladian house was built in 1735 and the park was enclosed and landscaped a few years later. House and park were used as the setting for Sir Walter Scott's ballad *Rokeby*. Its pride and joy is Velazquez's *Rokeby Venus*, which now hangs in the National Gallery in London, but many other paintings and a unique collection of needlework by Anne Morritt (1726-97) are on display in the compact buildings. To the east of the house, fourteenth-century Mortham Tower is glimpsed through the trees. It was the original home of the Rokeby family, but most of the tower and its Tudor additions are in ruins. Rokeby has been owned by the Morritt family since 1769 and is open to the public.

Continue along the road past Rokeby, and within site of the Tees, about 2 miles south-east of Barnard Castle, you will come to the ruins of **Egglestone Abbey**. Founded in the twelfth century by the Premonstratensian canons, it suffered the fate of almost all monasteries at the hands of Henry VIII's officers. Well sited, it sits above the flood level of the Tees near to where Thorsgill Beck flows into the main river. The setting is tranquil and much of the cruciform, aiseleless church still survives, especially the nave and chancel. The windows are Early English although the east window is thought to be later. Further monastic buildings on the site were converted to a farmhouse after the Dissolution. The ruins are maintained by English Heritage and access is either by road, (limited wheelchair access), or along one of the $1^3/_4$ mile riverside footpaths following either bank of the Tees downstream from Barnard Castle.

The Tees, may be followed downstream past a series of attractive riverside villages as far as Darlington. The first of these villages is

Whorlton, where terraced cottages with well-tended gardens follow the ascending street above the riverbank. The road crosses the Tees by a suspension bridge which has been in service since 1829. The hall and church are Victorian, but the church at least is built on Saxon foundations and there has been a village here since at least 1050, when it was documented as *Queorningtun*. Whorlton Lido is across the river where a veteran miniature locomotive pulls passengers on a 15in gauge railway. Picnic sites, childrens' corner, a London bus all help to make this a pleasant way of spending a sunny afternoon.

The A67 Barnard Castle-Darlington road skirts the northern edge of **Winston**, a charming spot that perches above a tree-lined stretch of the Tees. The parish church of St Andrew, though partly rebuilt in the last century, still retains many of its original thirteenth-century features.

Next along the A67 is **Gainford**; the old village is a grouping of Georgian houses above the River Tees built around a wide village green, and considered by many to be the most attractive in County Durham. The main road divides the old from the newer part of Gainford. The church is Early English, on the site of a Saxon monastery and, it is rumoured, built from stones taken from a Roman fort at nearby Piercebridge. Inside are memorials to the local gentry, notably Middletons, a family who owned Jacobean Gainford Hall at the west end of the village. About a mile upstream from the village, and only accessible on foot over rough ground, is Gainford Spa, a group of unpleasant smelling sulphur springs which can be detected from some distance! A little to the north along an unclassified road from Gainford is **Headlam**, a tiny village in a charming rural setting, a good vantage point for views of the north Pennine Moors across Teesdale. Headlam Hall, a privately owned Jacobean manor house stands on the southern outskirts of the village. High stone walls, broken only by an exquisite wrought-iron gate, surround the house and its gardens.

Roman engineers built a fort on the site of what eventually became **Piercebridge** . It guarded the crossing of the Tees by Dere Street, the arrow-straight road from York to Scotland by way of Hadrian's Wall. Excavation work on the site of the fort has revealed many interesting artifacts that are now on display in museums throughout the North-East. One recent discovery suggests that the Tees near Piercebridge was partly canalised in Roman times, giving rise to the theory that heavy goods were transported by barge rather than hauled by mules or oxen along the steeply graded roads.

A bridge carrying the B6275 — the modern Dere Street — is built over three stately arches and dates from 1789. The George Hotel in the main street has a clock that is said to be the one alluded to in Henry C. Work's song *My Grandfather's Clock*. It apparently stopped at the very moment of its owner's death.

A mile downstream **High Coniscliffe** — the name means King's Cliff — straddles the A67 high above the Tees. Its main street is lined with Georgian houses and cottages and the church spire is a landmark for miles from the south. Originally Saxon and Norman, it was rebuilt in 1846 in the Early English style and is dedicated to St Edwin, the Northumbrian king who did much to encourage the early spread of Christianity in his kingdom. Fragments of Saxon stonework and a Norman window remain from the original structure. There are interesting fifteenth-century chancel stalls, a twelfth-century tomb cover in the porch, as well as a late seventeenth-century monument to one of the Bowes family who lived at Thornton Hall. On a side lane of the B6279 Staindrop-Darlington road to the north, **Denton**, a cluster of whitewashed farm buildings and cottages, fits snugly around Cocker Beck in rolling countryside to the north-west of Darlington. The church, though much restored in the nineteenth century, is Norman and has some interesting medieval relics, especially a blue marble twelfth-century tombstone built into the vestry wall. Thornton Hall stands back from the B6279 roughly half way between Denton and Darlington. A tall, gabled structure, its design spans three centuries, beginning in the sixteenth.

Although **Darlington**'s south-western suburbs have encroached on to the north bank of the Tees, its centre developed around the River Skerne which joins the Tees 2 miles to the south of the town. The first impressions are of a mixture of Victorian houses partly dominated by an unattractive modern town centre surrounded by a fast inner-ring road. However, first impressions are not always correct for many of the older streets have escaped the developers' clutches. Known as 'gates' (from the Norse word for road or street), they follow a pattern which probably traces the line of tracks within the first Anglo-Saxon settlement, which later became an important market in Norman times.

Darlington's rapid expansion came with the development of the railway system. The first fare-paying steam-driven passenger trains ran from here to Stockton-on-Tees in 1825, an era commemorated by the North Road Station Museum off Northgate, where George Stephenson's original *Locomotion Number One* is on display alongside many other examples of railway memorabilia. The station — reminiscent of a Hampshire country gentleman's house — was redesigned in 1887 by the railway architect William Bell. The house where Edward Pease was born stands on the corner of Bull Wynd and Houndgate, opposite a row of Georgian houses. He championed steam locomotion as a means of carrying Durham coal to the Tees for shipping to London and the Continent.

The Wynd, one of the oldest streets in the town where there was once a bull ring, leads to the market place with the old market hall and Victorian town hall cheek by jowl. A splendid three-storeyed Georgian town house, Bennet House, a link with Darlington's earliest importance as a centre of commerce, stands in the Horse Market. Tubwell Row, on the north side of the market, houses the Darlington Museum with its collection of local, natural and social history items. The Civic Theatre is in the New Hippodrome, a building from the turn of the century in the original music hall tradition. The modern conversion is classed as one of the best examples of civic theatres in Britain.

St Cuthbert's Church is a splendid example of Early English architecture; dating from 1192 it probably replaced an earlier building. The church is on the west bank of the Skerne, at the head of a short riverside walk from the modern town centre.

Darlington is well served for public recreation with six parks and eighteen playing fields and open spaces. Nature trails are usually organized every summer and the annual Darlington Show is held each August in South Park.

In gently rolling countryside to the north of Darlington, the A6072 separates **Heighington** from its new town industrial neighbour Newton Aycliffe. Attractive groups of cottages and terraced houses line a series of wide sloping greens on either side of the Norman church. The pulpit with its six linenfold panels and brass memorials are particularly noteworthy. Heighington Hall, northeast of the church, is early eighteenth century and has some interesting stonework. The descendants of Captain Cumby, commander of HMS Royal Sovereign at the Battle of Trafalgar, still live at Trafalgar House, a pleasant nineteenth-century squire's house partly hidden behind high walls on the Aycliffe road. Redcliffe Hall is a mile to the north of the village. It is part sixteenth century and part nineteenth, a stone-gabled dwelling and once the home of the Surtees family, but now used as a school.

Returning again to the River Tees, **Hurworth-on-Tees** is another attractive riverside village. This is the eastern of three almost adjoining villages, Hurworth Place and Croft-on-Tees being the others, the latter being in North Yorkshire. Several fine Georgian houses are built around a long, bright village green where the parish church of All Saints has foundations which go back at least to the fifteenth century. Effigies in the church are said to be from nearby Neasham

Abbey, founded by Benedictine nuns and disolved by Henry VIII. The coal-owning Millbanke family pew stands boxlike on columns above the nave. William Emerson, an eccentric mathematical genius, was buried in the churchyard in 1782, his Hebrew and Latin epitaphs indicating his classical education. Hurworth's bay-windowed manor house, one of the finest dwellings lining the village green, was built in 1728; it is now a preparatory school.

Lewis Carroll, author of *Alice in Wonderland*, lived at **Croft-on-Tees** for 25 years. The two villages are connected by a seven-ribbed arch bridge which though strengthened and widened over the years (it now carries the A167), is basically the one built by Bishop Skirlaw in the early fourteenth century.

A row of cottages lining a green next to the Tees at **Neasham** are the successors of home farm cottages supporting an abbey which has long disappeared. The village is favoured with wide views up and down the Tees, especially south-east over the Sockburn peninsula. **Sockburn** is a tiny hamlet, the most southerly habitation in County Durham, which is at the end of a long peninsula created by a loop in the Tees. The red-brick Georgian farmhouse is where the Lakeland poet Wordsworth and his sister Mary were staying in 1799 when he met Mary Hutchinson, who was to become his wife.

Wordsworth also visited **Low Dinsdale**, a tiny hamlet to the north-east of Neasham marking a minor crossing of the Tees. The river twists and turns almost cutting back on itself, through the last of the countryside before industrial Teesside. Wordsworth and his sister came here to visit the sulphur springs and the hamlet once had a moment of fame as a spa. You can retrace Wordsworth's steps by following a delightful woodland path along the riverbank for about half a mile towards Middleton One Row. The sixteenth-century manor house, home of the Surtees family, is built on a mound above a series of dry moats, a reminder of the age of the site. Surtees memorials dating from the fourteenth century onwards decorate the church. Restored in the late nineteenth century, there has been a church on the same site since the twelfth century. The name Surtees means 'dweller by the Tees'.

Middleton One Row lines a gentle southerly bend of the Tees. In the eighteenth century it became a popular spa based on the sulphur springs first discovered by miners searching for outcropping coal. Today the village has unrivalled views south across the river and into the Vale of York.

Middleton St George straggles away from the Tees, and the Victorian restoration of an older church, in keeping with this apparent wish of the village to spread itself, stands almost aloof among fields. Incongruous pews inside it look rather like old-fashioned railway waiting room seats.

There are several Middletons in this widely spread parish; as well as One Row, there is also a Low Middleton and a West. Low Middleton Hall is about 2 miles to the south-east, an early eighteenth-century brick built house with ten sash windows overlooking its formal gardens.

Luckily for **Sadberge**, the A66 trunk road from Darlington to Middlesbrough bypasses it to the south, leaving behind an ancient village built on rising ground above rolling acres of farmland. Sadberge was once the centre of a 'wapentake' stretching from Middleton-in-Teesdale to Seaton Carew on the coast. Wapentakes were originally local assemblies that ruled areas of Viking settled territories and corresponded to 'hundreds' further south. At the time of Queen Victoria's Jubilee, the locals could still refer to her as 'Countess of Sadberge'.

Selected Walks

Widdybank Fell and Upper Teesdale
7 miles • Fairly strenuous • 4 hours
Map: Ordnance Survey Outdoor Leisure 1:25000 Series Sheet 31; Teesdale.
Rare semi-alpine flowers bloom beside the track near the start of this walk. It begins by Cow Green Reservoir which is reached at the end of a 3-mile side road off the B6277 at Langdon Beck in Upper Teesdale. The highlight for most will be the spectacular view of Cauldron Snout waterfall and then the long reach of Cow Green Reservoir backed by the highest summits of the Pennine chain. As part of the return leg of the walk follows a nature trail, try to collect a trail leaflet before leaving the car park.
From Cow Green car park, walk back for about $2^1/_2$ miles down the moorland road you have just driven along. Ignoring the side road left, walk on until a farm lane on the right is reached, opposite a barn. Turn right and walk down the winding lane to Widdybank Farm. Go through the farmyard and follow a footpath down to the riverbank. Turn right and walk upstream beside the Tees. After about 2 miles, the path crosses a boulder field at the foot of a dolerite outcrop called Falcon Clints. At the junction with a side stream, turn right and climb the rocky path beside Cauldron Snout *(NB Take care, the rocks can be slippery after rain)*. Join a metalled track and climb to the right of the dam wall then continue along the track until the car park is reached.

Low Force

2 miles • Easy • $1\frac{1}{2}$ hours

Map: Ordnance Survey Outdoor Leisure Series 1:25000 Sheet 31; Teesdale.

Park at the Bowlees visitor centre on the B6277 about 3 miles north-west of Middleton-in-Teesdale.

Cross the main road and follow the signposted field path down to the river and Wynch Bridge. Cross the suspension bridge and turn right, walking upstream for about 300yd to view the rapids at Low Force. Retrace your steps and follow the river downstream for about three quarters of a mile until you reach Scoberry Bridge. Cross this and on the other side of the river go diagonally right across two fields to a footbridge across a side stream. **Do not cross this bridge**, but bear left beside a wood until you reach a farm building. Follow the access track, still at the side of the wood and on reaching the road, cross over and again follow a path next to a continuation of the woodland belt. Turn left to reach the visitor centre.

The walk can be extended by following the waymarked path for about half a mile upstream to Gibson Cave, a pretty waterfall-backed dell with a picnic site.

Egglestone Abbey

3 miles • Easy • 2 hours

Map: Ordnance Survey Outdoor Leisure Series 1:25000 Sheet 31; Teesdale.

The tranquil ruins of this ancient abbey are the highlight of an attractive riverside walk from Barnard Castle. From the market cross in Barnard Castle, walk down the main street and cross the footbridge. Turn left and follow the riverside path. Bear right around a caravan park and cross a series of fields until a road is reached. Follow this to the access to the abbey. After viewing the abbey, rejoin the road and follow it to the junction with another road. Turn left at the junction and go over the bridge across the Tees. On the far side, turn left along a riverside footpath and follow it until it joins a farm lane. Continue along the lane, past the farm and into Barnard Castle.

A Scenic Drive Through the Upper Dales

62 miles • 100km

As a number of single track and unfenced roads are used on this drive, please take extra care and be ready for oncoming traffic or straying sheep. The drive is through part of the North Pennines Area of Outstanding Natural Beauty and visits a number of interesting villages along the way. It starts and finishes in Barnard Castle.

From Barnard Castle take the B6278 through Eggleston (ancient pack horse bridge) and B6282 to Middleton-in-Teesdale (one-time headquarters of the London Lead Company; attractive main street, shops and cafés). Take the B6277 along Teesdale to Bowlees (visitor centre, picnic sites and riverside walks). Drive on to High Force (small entrance fee for the waterfall, pub). At Langdon Beck turn right and follow the narrow unfenced moorland road over Langdon Common and down into Weardale. (Possible diversion left to Killhope Wheel Lead Mining Centre at the dale head.) Turn right along the A689 and drive through a series of small villages (Stanhope is particularly interesting) to Wolsingham (cafés, pubs, shops, attractive old houses). Turn right in the centre and follow a steep unclassified road south up the valley side. Take the left fork after a little over a mile, then right again at the next. Go downhill almost into Bedburn, but do not cross the bridge. Turn right and follow a side road into Hamsterley Forest; pay the toll and go along the Forest Drive (walks, picnic sites, wildlife). Leaving the forest bear right along a moorland road, then left on reaching the B6282. Go through the straggling villages of Woodland and Copley (ignore a turning right at Copley). At the foot of a steep descent into a narrow valley, turn right (watch out for oncoming traffic at this tricky junction), and ignoring a left turn at the top of the hill, go through Burnt Houses (pub here) and past a large area of woodland to the main A688. Turn right along the main road to drive past Raby Castle (medieval castle and deerpark) and follow the road through Staindrop (pub and shops) to Barnard Castle.

5

CLEVELAND

A lthough the name given to Cleveland has links with an ancient sub-division of Northumbria the present boundary was created by bureaucracy. Until 1974, towns north of the Tees were part of County Durham and those to the south were in the North Riding of Yorkshire. At a stroke, the new county of Cleveland was created, the 'Ridings' were ignored and people whose ancestors had for centuries been from Durham or Yorkshire, now found themselves Clevelanders. In this final chapter the county will be described by moving down the Tees from Stockton before moving on to Middlesbrough, Billingham and the ancient part of Hartlepool. Then the jumble of towns and villages south of the river will be explored, along to the coast.

There has been a market at **Stockton-on-Tees** since medieval times and the town developed as a port in the eighteenth century. Shipping no longer comes so far up the Tees, but there are still traces of the old warehouses and narrow riverside alleyways off the spacious High Street, close to Green Dragon Yard. This area has been recreated into a spacious exhibition centre based on the Green Dragon Gallery and the intimate Georgian Theatre.

The railway era brought almost overnight prosperity to the town, an event usually linked with the opening of the Stockton and Darlington Railway in 1825, the world's first fare-paying passenger steam railway. The old ticket office in Bridge Street has been preserved as a museum commemorating this historic railway. Modern Stockton is a mixture, not always comfortable, of old and new. The town hall and market cross both date from the mid-1700s, but even though they and the parish church are of similar age and make an attractive group, the town tends to be dominated by ill-conceived tower blocks, its mad whirl of ring roads and complex river cross-

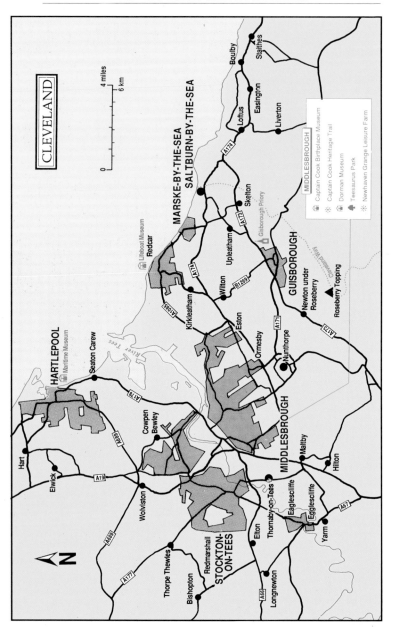

CLEVELAND

0   4 miles

6 km

N

HARTLEPOOL

MARSKE-BY-THE-SEA

SALTBURN-BY-THE-SEA

Boulby

Staithes

Easington

Liverton

Loftus

A174

Skelton

A173

Gisborough Priory

Redcar

Lifeboat Museum

Upleatham

Wilton

B1269

GUISBOROUGH

Newton under Roseberry

Cleveland Way

Roseberry Topping

Kirkleatham

A1085

Eston

Ormesby

Nunthorpe

A171

A174

Seaton Carew

Maritime Museum

River Tees

A178

River Tees

MIDDLESBROUGH

Cowpen Bewley

Maltby

Hilton

Hart

Elwick

A19

Wolviston

A689

Thornaby-on-Tees

Egglescliffe

Eaglescliffe

A67

Yarm

Thorpe Thewles

A177

Bishopton

Redmarshall

STOCKTON-ON-TEES

Elton

Longnewton

A66

MIDDLESBROUGH

1 Captain Cook Birthplace Museum
2 Captain Cook Heritage Trail
3 Dorman Museum
4 Teesaurus Park
5 Newhaven Grange Leisure Farm

The Transporter Bridge, Middlesbrough

ings. Stockton has changed radically over the years and has spread to enclose and suburbanise several surrounding towns and villages. Among them is **Elton**, south of the A66. Elton Hall, former home of the Ropners, looks like a Queen Anne style building, but was in fact built in this century and is now used as offices. The church is a Victorian reconstruction of a Norman building. Its interior is noteworthy, especially the colourful rood screen.

The industrial suburb of **Thornaby-on-Tees** is hemmed-in by dual carriageways in the north and east and the river to the west. What is left of the original village surrounds a wide green, watched over by its eleventh-century church of St Peter ad Vincula, and is now a conservation area. The Green farmhouse is of the eighteenth century at the rear, but its front dates from the nineteenth. Sundial House has the date 1621 displayed on the front wall. The area cordonned by the triangle created by the A66, A19 and A1130, once the site of Stockton Race Course, is, together with a shopping complex, now the largest sports and leisure complex in the United Kingdom.

South-west along the A135 from Stockton is the burgeoning industrial suburb of **Eaglescliffe**, where only a handful of older cottages survive among the modern developments. Preston Hall

Museum stands beside the A135 to the north of the town, and here the social history of the region is depicted through the use of period streets and reconstructed rooms. As the Stockton and Darlington Railway ran along the boundary of the park, transport is an important theme in the museum. Indoor galleries have displays ranging from toys to costume and pewter. There are play areas, a small zoo and riverside walks in a parkland setting.

The A135 separates Eaglescliffe from **Egglescliffe**. Similar in name, but not in character, this is a pleasant backwater of red-tiled farms and cottages centred around a village green, on rising ground above the meandering Tees. Its elevated position gives it wide views of the Vale of York to the south, across the rooftops of neighbouring Yarm. The river is crossed by a fifteenth-century road bridge and a brick railway viaduct with forty-three arches. The parish church of St Mary is mainly Perpendicular in style with a good array of woodwork (notably a barrel roof of oak) and an eighteenth-century three-decker pulpit.

Cleveland's history is condensed into the little town of **Yarm**, which is built on a narrow peninsula formed by a tight bend in the Tees. At one time Yarm was a sizeable port, dealing with farm produce, coal and lead, with shipping coming so far up the river to avoid the inhospitable saltflats and marshes where Middlesbrough and Billingham now stand.

Before the rise of Middlesbrough, Yarm was the most important town on the River Tees. Elegant Georgian merchants' houses built on the prosperity of its industry still dominate the end of the High Street, but the industry disappeared with the growth of the new towns closer to the sea.

The ancient bridge dates from 1400, when Bishop Skirlaw of Durham ordered its construction. The parish church of St Mary Magdalene is mostly as it was rebuilt in 1730. There are, however, much older parts around the west end; of special note is the curious 'fish eye' window. A Dominican friary first stood on the site of the Friarage, built in 1770, the only relic of the older building being a Tudor dovecot. The original Methodist chapel in Capel Wynd was built in 1736, a building much admired by John Wesley when he visited Yarm on his great treks around the country. Twentieth-century Yarm is a small town with a delightful mixture of buildings lining its wide, cobble-edged main street. The town is made all the more interesting by a trail following its old streets and 'Wynds', which takes in the best features. Being on what was an important coach road to the north, the High Street has its fair share of interesting old inns. The eighteenth-century George and Dragon was used as a meeting place for promoters of the Stockton and Darlington Railway, but it is perhaps the town hall that generates the most interest from an architectural point of view. Built in 1710 in the Dutch style, it was originally a court house and is now, since Yarm merged with Stockton, the meeting place for the local council.

Rich farmland fills the segment created by the A66 and A19. The one long main street of **Longnewton** leaves the busy A66 about half way between Stockton and Darlington. Modern housing blends well with older properties in the village associated with the Durham coal-owning family, the Vanes. A grandiose vaulted mausoleum guards the mortal remains of many of them in a church, built in 1856, of otherwise uninteresting appearance. Their home, Long Newton Hall, was to the west of the village street, but only the enclosure wall remains. Behind the church is Longnewton's finest building, the seventeenth- and eighteenth-century rectory.

Other villages in this green-belt are **Bishopton** on a quiet winding road 4 miles north-west of Stockton, where an ancient site to the south of the village known as Castle Hill covers 7 acres with double ditches and a 40ft-high mound or bailey. **Redmarshall** is $1^1/_2$ miles to the east, an exclusive village much favoured by commuting Teesside executives. The parish church is tucked away behind the road to Bishopton. Partly Norman, it has later additions dating from the thirteenth and fifteenth centuries. A Victorian rectory, dominated by its tall gables, stands to the east of the church. The Ship Inn, a popular venue is near by; it dates from the eighteenth century and the steeply sloping pantiled roof is its most eye-catching feature.

The road north-east from the latter reaches **Thorp Thewles** where the roar of traffic thundering along the A177 is thankfully well to its east. Part of the track of the old Stockton to Sunderland Railway north of Thorpe Thewles has been converted into a long-distance footpath and cycle way, known as the Castle Eden Walkway. The track passes through a number of cuttings that hold snow in winter and has become a popular cross-country ski track when conditions permit.

Served by a side road and bordered by the A177 and A689, **Wynyard Park** is about 3 miles to the north of Stockton. The house, park and farmland are sheltered from public gaze by cleverly-planted mature woodlands. The house was erected in 1841, but there has been a manor house on the same site since the Middle Ages. It is built on the grand scale: a six-columned Corinthian portico dominates an entrance that leads to great and sumptuous galleries and the state room. The latter overlooks Wynyard's formal gardens, from whose terrace a lake winds towards woodland.

James Cook (1728-79), navigator and explorer, was born at Marton, now a suburb of **Middlesbrough**. His birthplace is marked by a granite plinth in Stewart Park, at the start of the Captain Cook Heritage Trail. The trail, with its eye-catching symbols and plaques, visits places associated with Cook's early life in Cleveland. The Birthplace Museum in Stewart Park explains with dioramas and in sound the story of James Cook and his exploits and discoveries around the world. Plants from many of the tropical countries he visited are housed in an adjacent conservatory.

Other museums and places of interest in the area are: the Dorman Museum, which has a collection of pottery made in the district and exhibits that follow the development of the town; the Middles- brough Art Gallery, which usually has exhibitions of paintings by modern and past British artists covering four centuries from the sixteenth; Teesaurus Park is an imaginative recreation of dinosaur models on an elevated mound on reclaimed riverside land; Newham Grange Leisure Farm is to the south of the town, just off the B1365, where visitors are encouraged to walk round and study farm animals in a working environment. A nineteenth-century vet's shop, farmhouse kitchen and a collection of rare breeds complete the attractions on offer at the farm.

The residential suburb of **Nunthorpe** on the south-east side of Middlesbrough is notable for the seventeenth-century Nunthorpe Hall, built within the grounds of a twelfth-century nunnery. The house is now an old people's home. Its near neighbour, a little closer to Middlesbrough, is **Ormesby** where the oldest part is to the south and above the A174. The church is late nineteenth century, but medieval memorials denote its earlier foundations. Ormesby Hall stands at the head of a landscaped park and is an eighteenth-century reconstruction of a house owned by the Pennyman family from 1600. There is some excellent Adam plasterwork and an attractive stable block designed by John Carr of York. Both hall and park are owned by the National Trust and maintained jointly with the local authority.

Of all the ancient villages which were swallowed to become suburbs of Middlesbrough, **Eston** to the east of the town centre can claim to have the oldest. Its history goes back to at least the Bronze Age when there was a camp on top of Eston Nab, a northern outlier of the Cleveland Hills. Footpaths from a car park and picnic site at Ten Acre Bank, south of the A174, climb Eston Moor to the top of the Nab where the view across Teesside contrasts starkly with the rolling heather moors to the south.

Beyond the traffic island marking the junction of the A174 and

Totem pole at the Captain Cook Museum, Marton

A1053, the small 'estate' village of **Wilton** clusters around Wilton Castle. The present castle was built in 1807 by Sir John Lowther, and is now the property of ICI Ltd. The village church dedicated to St Cuthbert is basically twelfth century, but was 'improved' in the nineteenth. Several interesting old buildings are near by, despite intrusions by the Middlesbrough commuter belt: seventeenth-century Lackenby Hall has some fine mullioned windows; Lazenby farmhouse was built in the early part of the nineteenth century and is now a private residence.

Eston Nab and other prominent heights featuring in this part of Cleveland are relics of the last ice age. They became isolated summits along the northern edge of the Cleveland Hills, protruding from the ice sheet which covered the rest of the district. **Roseberry Topping** to the south is another of these hills. It marks the boundary between Cleveland and North Yorkshire and is known affectionately as Cleveland's 'Matterhorn'. At 1,051ft the hill is the most prominent feature in the surrounding landscape and has been used to signal important events, ranging from the coming of the Armada to the Coronation of Queen Elizabeth II.

Mesolithic and Neolithic herdsmen sheltered in safety on its summit and left behind traces of their simple technology. Throughout the centuries the hill's name has changed from Othensberg (Odin's Hill) in 1119 to Onesburg in 1231, becoming Osburye Toppyne in 1591, the forerunner of the modern title. Footpaths reach this airy vantage point from several directions, One starts in the cluster of houses on either side of the A173 known prosaically as Newton under Roseberry.

Small villages sit at the head of the tidal reach and beyond the salt marshes of the north bank of the Tees' mouth. **Cowpen Bewley** is almost surrounded by Billingham to its south-west, but the village has retained its agricultural base since the eighteenth-century. The regular layout of farms and cottages on either side of a wide green follows a pattern established soon after the Norman Conquest. Village Farm and Little Neuk Farm Cottage, dating from the early eighteenth century, and seventeenth century Ivy House, are its most notable buildings. Despite the spread of modern industry on esturial marshlands, waders and other migrant wildfowl from Scandinavia and Siberia, and even further afield, still visit this corner of the North-East. Cowpen Nature Reserve which lies off the A178 Hartlepool road, has been made into a haven for these visitors.

Wolviston is on the northern outskirts of Billingham, tucked away beneath a complex of busy roundabouts and flyovers. The village has a proud reputation for winning the Britain in Bloom competition many times over. A well-kept village green surrounded by attractive gardens makes a pleasant oasis in Teesside's industrial belt.

The A19(T) follows a sinuous course north from Billingham, bypassing towns and villages on its way to Sunderland. About 4 miles north of the intersection with the A689, and reached by a dangerous right turn off the A19, two side roads lead down to **Elwick**, a picture-postcard village of old cottages and a seventeenth-century hall in a pleasant rural setting. The main street is lined with a narrow greensward on either side and backed by attractive buildings. The village was established long before the Norman Conquest, part of the wapentake of *Sadberge*. The church stands a little aloof on a prominent rise away from the centre of the village, an interesting mixture of styles dating from the thirteenth, seventeenth and nineteenth centuries. Look for two small, intriguing Saxon carvings on either side of the chancel arch.

A slip road leaves the A19 to join the A179 Hartlepool road, where in a little over a mile a side road leads into **Hart**, a small peaceful community in a rural setting, built on gently rising ground.

This elevated situation gives the village wide views over the surrounding fields towards the North Sea. The Church of St Mary Magdalen is seventh century and was originally the mother church of Hartlepool; and though the village remained small, its offspring grew. Very little remains of the original Saxon church, but there is a Saxon sundial and a rather plain looking Norman font, together with another more ornate font dating from the fifteenth century; the rest of the church is seventeenth and nineteenth century. The name of Brewery Farm indicates the part-time occupation of its previous owners.

Hartlepool is based on ancient foundations and was the first fortified harbour on the North-East coast. The old town occupies a hook-like promontory formed by Parton Rocks and behind which is a natural harbour. Streets in this part of the town are still laid out within the original pattern dictated by a defensive wall, built to the orders of King John in the thirteenth century to keep seaborne Scots attackers at bay. When finished, the wall with its ten watch towers was a formidable barrier, only falling into disuse after its capture and destruction by the Scots during the Civil War.

The prosperity of Hartlepool as a port grew in the mid-1800s, when a railway linked it to the Durham coalfields. Victoria Dock, its main harbour for coal shipments, was opened in 1840, but coal is no longer a major export. A dignified Victorian Customs House still watches movements in and out of the old harbour, protected to the south by a long curving pier, but until recently it was looking out on to a scene of great dereliction. Part of the docks are now put to use for the reconstruction of old ships. HMS *Warrior* was restored here and with the refurbishment of ships like the Victorian paddle steamer *Wingfield Castle* and the 172-year old frigate *Foudroyant* are beginning to create an exciting collection of vintage ships. These ships, together with a £150 million marina, town houses and luxury flats, are bringing life back to what had become a derelict wilderness.

The Maritime Museum is in Northgate and the Gray Museum and Art Gallery concentrates on scenes of local industry and landscapes. Its name commemorates Sir William Gray, one of the founding fathers of Hartlepool's prosperity. Another was Ralph Ward Jackson, whose name is remembered in the Ward Jackson Park on the eastern outskirts. Hartlepool's parks are a subject of justifiable local pride, usually a blaze of colour throughout the summer. The power station has an exhibition entitled 'Generations of Industry'.

Seaton Carew, to the south-east of West Hartlepool, marks the centre of miles of clean open sandy beaches backed by dunes with the north bank of the Tees to their south. Formerly a fishing village, it

Saltburn Beach

once had hopes of becoming a highly select holiday resort, the northern equivalent of Littlehampton or Bognor Regis. Rows of colourful fishermen's cottages, attractive Regency and late nineteenth-century houses line the sea front and the modest village green. Despite the nearness of industry, the village retains its air of a failed, but still genteel, watering place. The flat hard sand is popular with horse riders and sand yachtsmen, as well as the more traditional day visitors. North Gare Breakwater, beyond sand dunes lining the mouth of the Tees, is an ideal vantage point for watching shipping leaving and entering the river.

Guisborough and the Coast

Guisborough was the 'capital' of Cleveland in Anglo-Saxon times, but now it is part of the Borough of Langbaurgh. A busy town, part market, part dormitory for Teesside commuters, the town spreads from wide and cobble-verged Westgate, once the scene of busy markets, but now lined by attractive shops and cafés. At the far end of Westgate, a gate in a wall near the parish church leads into what at first glance is a garden. Smooth lawns and herb gardens now cover most of Gisborough Priory. Almost 900 years old, the outline of the nave and chancel are still recognizable and lead the eye towards the tracery of the once magnificent east window. A place of absolute serenity, the only complete relic is a medieval octagonal dovecot which still attracts these gentle birds. Gisborough Priory is maintained by English Heritage and is open daily at standard English Heritage times.

Like the priory, the 'u' is dropped in Gisborough Hall; it stands a little to the east across fields beyond the priory. It was the home of the Chaloner family who founded the town hospital, but were punished for being supporters of Charles I during the Civil War.

Tockett's Mill is in a wooded dell about a mile east from Guisborough along a side road off the A173. Cleveland's only surviving watermill, it is owned by a private trust and open to the public on advertised days.

Moving north along the B1269 towards the coast, **Kirkleatham**, about $3^1/_2$ miles north of Guisborough, was once surrounded by a deerpark, but now by the busy A174 and A1042. Despite the traffic and also its proximity to ICI's Wilton chemical works, the village manages to hold on to much of its former tranquillity. Recorded as *Westlidum* in the Domesday Book the village was owned by William de Percy in the eleventh-century, then by the Lumley family, and in 1623 it was bought by John Turner of Guisborough, who had made his fortune from mining alum. Of the once grand house, the centre of this estate, only the stable block remains and the Old Hall Museum is next door to the local school. Exhibits cover a wide range of scientific discoveries, especially related to Cleveland. A children's play area, an aviary and an attractively laid out garden complete this imaginative establishment.

Sir William Turner founded the almshouses, now known as the Turner Hospital and Kirkleatham's finest buildings, in 1676 for the accommodation of 'ten poor men, ten poor women, ten poor boys and ten poor girls'. Although the definition of poor has changed radically since then, the almshouses are still used for their original purpose. The present buildings date from 1742, following their remodelling by Turner's great-nephew Chomley Turner, who also paid for the chapel. Nearby is St Cuthbert's Church which has stood on the same site for over 900 years, although the present building dates from 1763. The church has several interesting brasses and a Turner mausoleum as its main features.

Redcar was once a tiny fishing village, but it grew when the railway reached it in 1846, bringing early Middlesbrough commuters and also holidaymakers to enjoy its golden sands. The town is unique in having a racecourse almost in its centre and thoroughbreds can usually be seen exercising on the firm sands close to fishing boats drawn up on the harbourless beach. Flat race meetings are held between early March and the end of October. Redcar's amenities are centred on the 9 miles of almost uninterrupted sandy beaches from the mouth of the Tees to the foot of Hunt Cliff, beyond Saltburn-by-the-Sea. Inland, the town has a large modern leisure centre, a boating lake and swimming pool. The Lifeboat Museum on King Street has as its main exhibit the *Zetland*, the oldest surviving lifeboat. Built in 1800 by Greathead, it saved hundreds of lives on this treacherous North-East coast.

Marske-by-the-Sea is another town that grew from a fishing village, but its streets appear to turn their back on the sea. As with many other towns and villages on this exposed section of coast, there is no harbour and boats are launched from a slipway. Sturdy old stone fishermen's cottages and later ironstone miners' houses near the High Street can still be found tucked away between the shopping centre and modern housing developments. One of them is a charming sixteenth-century cruck cottage in High Street known as Winkey's Castle. It now houses a small but varied collection of local exhibits related to fishing and mining. The parish church is Victorian, but a Norman font and a thirteenth-century wayside cross indicate its earlier foundations. Marske Hall is behind it; built in 1625 it is now a Cheshire Home. Captain Cook's father is buried in St

Staithes

Germain's, on the clifftop east of the town centre. The church is abandoned and was demolished in 1960, with only the tower left as a marker for shipping.

Trains no longer deposit holidaymakers inside the foyer of **Saltburn-by-the-Sea**'s Zetland Hotel. The station, along with the hotel and town, has had to adapt to changing fashions of holidaymaking. Gone are its ornate canopies and comfortable waiting rooms, their place taken up by a shopping precinct, while small two-coach diesel trains take commuters to Middlesbrough. The railway brought prosperity to Saltburn in 1861 and for a time it enjoyed a vogue as a 'superior' type of resort. Planned as one of the leading watering places in Britain, the deep-cut ravine of Riftswood marked a sort of frontier beyond which ironstone miners from nearby villages were forbidden to pass. The wooded valley has an Italianate garden and secluded footpaths lead down to the seashore, where a miniature railway and playing fields are a more up-to-date innovation. The deep ravine was once crossed by a narrow elevated footbridge, known as Halfpenny Bridge from the cost of its toll; sadly it became a liability a few years ago and was demolished. At the opposite end of the promenade, another wooded ravine, Hazel Grove, more natural than Riftswood, is again followed by an easy footpath.

Saltburn has the only pier on the North-East coast; once 1,400ft long, it has been reduced to its present 600ft by storm and accidental ramming in 1924 by a ship, the *Ovenberg*. Saltburn's other unique feature is the inclined tramway opposite the pier entrance. It is the successor to a rickety, hoistlike contraption, built in 1870 to lift passengers 150ft from the promenade to the town. The original and potentially lethal structure of timber and guy ropes was demolished in 1883 and replaced by the present water-operated tramway.

The oldest part of the town is the small group of cottages now incorporated as part of the Ship Inn beneath Cat Nab. Once it was the haunt of smugglers whose activities, despite the ever watchful eye of the excisemen, brought illicit supplies of wines and spirits into Cleveland. There was a Roman signal station on Hunt Cliff above Cat Nab; its last occupants were murdered, possibly by Vikings, and their bodies dumped in a well. Coastal erosion has claimed the site, but a plaque on the present hilltop describes the building.

 The Cleveland Way, a 93-mile long-distance footpath, follows the western and northern edge of the North York Moors from Helmsley. It continues along the Cleveland escarpment above Guisborough, then joins the coast at Saltburn and follows it south to Filey Brig.

Upleatham never developed to the same degree as its neighbours during the ironstone mining boom, and as a result has returned more easily to its rural origins. Stone cottages, which give the village its character, look across the wooded valley of Skelton Beck towards eighteenth-century Skelton Castle nestling amidst its parkland. The village church of St Andrew's is said to be the smallest in England. Only 17ft 8in by 13ft, it is part of a larger twelfth-century building which had a battlemented tower added in 1644. The main feature inside the church is its attractive twelfth-century font.

Miners' cottages dating from the ironstone boom of the 1800s mix haphazardly with older properties in **Skelton**, the central village in this elevated complex. Most of the village is built around the 300ft contour and the land falls steeply to the east; there are fine views of the North Sea about 2 miles away. William the Conqueror granted Robert de Brus land in Cleveland and Skelton Castle became the family stronghold. It was rebuilt as a castellated mansion in 1794. The grounds are open once a year on Daffodil Sunday (variable, but advertised). An old well and village cross remain from days when Skelton held a village fair every Sunday in the local churchyard.

The main road climbs steeply out of Kilton Beck to **Loftus**, where agriculture has regained its ascendance over industry. Much of the old part of the town can be seen by following the short Loftus Dam Walk which follows the old street pattern to the dam and Loftus Mill, now a private house, but once an important amenity to the town. A leaflet describing the walk is available locally.

The remote and tiny hamlet of **Handale** is at the end of a deep, wooded valley south of Loftus, where there is the site of a former Cistercian abbey. Footpaths and lanes link it with **Liverton** on the B1366 from Loftus. Farms and cottages line its single street and the elvated position affords good seaward views across the intervening countryside. The church, dedicated to St Michael, was founded in the twelfth century, but altered early in the twentieth. Its finest relic from the past is the Norman chancel arch.

Livertons Waterwheel Inn indicates its name by a huge wheel over the entrance. Liverton Mill, a link with the agricultural past of the village, stands in the densely wooded valley bottom at the end of a side road a mile west of the village. Scaling Dam, 4 miles away on the edge of the moors, at the side of the A171 is stocked with fish; angling is available by day permit and there is also a picnic site.

Reached by a moorland road north from the dam and straddling the A174, Northumbria's other **Easington** (the other is near Peterlee in County Durham), sits on a hilltop site half way between Loftus and Staithes in North Yorkshire. The parish church of All Saints was established in Anglo-Saxon times, but the present building dates from 1888. A farmhouse stands close by, on the site of an ancient moat marking the position of a medieval manor house. Several other old buildings can be found mainly on the south side of the village.

A minor road roughly parallel to and north of the A174, crosses the highest part of the North-East coast to reach the cluster of houses that make up **Boulby**. The village was once the scene of intensive mining for alum and eighteenth-century smugglers found this remote section of coastline, an ideal place for their illicit deals in wines and spirits and other contraband. Boulby Cliff, the highest along the coast (679ft), rises from a rocky foreshore where fossils can be found at low tide.

To finish this extensive tour of Northumbria, it is necessary to stray a little way over the border into North Yorkshire to **Staithes**, purely on the strength of its links with Cleveland's most famous son, the navigator and explorer Captain James Cook. A side road, just in North Yorkshire, leaves the A174 and descends steeply past rows of un-prepossessing houses to a car park. From here you must walk downhill into the oldest part of the village, to where quaint fishermen's cottages cluster around the harbourside Cod and Lobster Inn. Traditionally designed cobles, a fishing boat whose ancestry is linked with Viking longships, shelter in Roxby Beck below Cowbar Nab and where the ghost of a headless girl is said to walk. Many of the older women still wear a starched frilled lace fishwife's bonnet and many of the locals speak a dialect unique to this ancient fishing harbour where James Cook was apprenticed to a draper. The coast now points the way southwards to the North York Moors.

Tips for Overseas Visitors to Britain

Tourist Offices

Can help with most travel information. Many will book accommodation, and it is often worthwhile writing to those listed in this book before you depart.

Currency/Credit Cards

The units of currency are pounds (£) and pence (p). Most major credit cards, especially VISA and MASTERCARD (Access), are widely accepted. Money can be changed at banks and at bureaux de change in major cities.

Driving Regulations

1   Speed limits: built-up areas 30mph (48kph)
    Approach to built-up areas 40mph (64kph)
    Motorways 70mph (113kph)
    Dual Carriageways 70mph (113kph)
    De-restricted sign (black diagonal stripe on white background) actually indicates a maximum speed of 60mph (97kph).
2   Age restrictions: drivers must be over 17.
3   Driving is on the left-hand side of the road.
4   The wearing of front and rear seat belts is compulsory.
5   Fuel: many fuel stations are self-service. The opening times vary, but many stay open until about 8pm and some for 24 hours. Lead-free petrol is widely available.

Car Hire

The major car rental groups (eg Hertz, Avis etc) operate from most cities and airports. There are also many smaller firms, and large garages often hire cars. Details of these and many other services are to be found in the local classified telephone directories (*Yellow Pages*).

Public Transport

Provision varies greatly from area to area, and it is best to check locally where you are staying. Tickets for long-distance travel are available from railway/bus stations. For shorter journeys tickets are available on buses, and sometimes on trains.

Banks

Generally open from 9.30am-3.30pm. Some stay open later and some open on Saturday mornings.

Shops, Post Offices etc

1   General opening hours are 9am-5.30pm, but many supermarkets and some smaller shops stay open later.
2   Most provisions can be obtained from supermarkets, but many specialised smaller shops (eg bakeries, butchers) are also available.
3   Stamps are available in 1st and 2nd class for letters/postcards. They can be purchased at post offices and some shops (eg newsagents).

Telephones

Most public telephones take all coins from 2p to £1. Phone cards are also available from post offices (there are separate phone boxes in which to use these).

Climate

The British weather is changeable throughout the year! The warmest months are usually July and August, but June and September can be drier. Generally, the west is warmer and wetter and the east colder and drier; the north is colder than the south. However, these variations are fairly small. A good mixture of clothes is advisable.

Emergencies

Phone 999 (free) for police, fire and ambulance services.

Religion

The 'official' religion is Church of England, but many others are widely practised.

National Holidays

Banks, post offices and many shops close for several days at Christmas; also on New Year's Day, Easter Monday, May Day Bank Holiday (first Monday in May), Spring Bank Holiday (last Monday in May) and Late Summer Bank Holiday (last Monday in August).

Pets

Quarantine requirements are very long, so visitors do not usually bring their pets.

FURTHER INFORMATION

Abbeys, Castles and Other Historic Buildings

EH - English Heritage
NT - National Trust

Auckland Castle Deer House, Bishop Auckland (EH)
In Bishop Auckland Park, just north of town centre on A689
Open: park — usually daylight hours. Chapel and state rooms open May-September.

Aydon Castle (EH)
1 mile north-east of Corbridge, on minor road off B6321 or A68
☎ (0434) 632450
Open: Good Friday or beginning April-end September, daily 10am-6pm.

Barnard Castle (EH)
In Barnard Castle
☎ (0833) 38212
Open: Good Friday or beginning April-end September, daily 10am-6pm; beginning October-Maundy Thursday or end March, Tuesday-Sunday 10am-4pm. Closed 24-26 December and 1 January.

Berwick Barracks (EH)
The parade, off Church Street, Berwick town centre
☎ (0289) 304493
Open: Good Friday or beginning April-end September, daily 10am-6pm; beginning October-Maundy Thursday or end March, Tuesday-Sunday 10am-4pm; closed 24-26 December and 1 January.

Berwick-upon-Tweed Castle (EH)
Adjacent to Berwick railway station, west of town centre; accessible also from riverbank.
Open: any reasonable time.

Berwick-upon Tweed Ramparts (EH)
Open: any reasonable time.

Bessie Surtees House (EH)
41-44 Sandhill, Newcastle upon Tyne
☎ (091) 261 1585
North regional headquarters of English Heritage.
Open: all the year, including Mondays in winter.

Black Middens Bastle House (EH)
200yd north of minor road 7 miles north-west of Bellingham; access also along minor road from A68. OS Map 80; ref NY774900.
Open: any reasonable time.

Bowes Castle (EH)

A quarter of a mile west of Bowes on A66, 4 miles west of Barnard Castle. Open: any reasonable time.

Brinkburn Priory (EH)

$4^1/_2$ mile south-east of Rothbury off B6334
☎ (066570) 628
Open: Good Friday or beginning April-end September, daily 10am-6pm.

Dunstanburgh Castle (Joint EH and NT)

8 miles north-east of Alnwick, on footpaths from Craster or Embleton
☎ (066576) 231
Open: Good Friday or beginning April-end September, daily 10am-6pm; beginning October-Maundy Thursday or end March, Tuesday-Sunday 10am-4pm; closed 24-26 December, 1 January.

Edlingham Castle (EH)

At east end of Edlingham village, on minor road off B6341, 6 miles south-west of Alnwick.
Open: any reasonable time.

Egglestone Abbey (EH)

1 mile south of Barnard Castle on minor road off B6277
Open: any reasonable time.

Etal Castle (EH)

In Etal village, 8 miles south-west of Berwick
Open: any reasonable time.

Finchdale Priory (EH)

3 miles north-east of Durham, on minor road off A167
Open: Good Friday or beginning April-end September, daily 10am-6pm; beginning October-Maundy Thursday or end March, Tuesday-Sunday 10am-4pm; closed 24-26 December, 1 January.

Gisborough Priory (EH)

In Guisborough town centre, next to the parish church
☎ (0287) 38301
Open: Good Friday or beginning April-end September, daily 10am-6pm; beginning October-Maundy Thursday or end March, Tuesday-Sunday 10am-4pm; closed 24-26 December, 1 January.

Hylton Castle (EH)

$3^3/_4$ miles west of Sunderland
Open: Good Friday or beginning April-end September, daily 10am-6pm; beginning October-Maundy Thursday or end March, Tuesday-Sunday 10am-4pm; closed 24-26 December, 1 January.

Lindisfarne Priory (EH)

On Holy Island, reached at low tide by causeway
☎ (028989) 200
Open: Good Friday or beginning April-end September, daily 10am-6pm; beginning October-Maundy Thursday or end March, Tuesday-Sunday 10am-4pm; closed 24-26 December, 1 January.

Norham Castle (EH)

Norham village, $6^1/_2$ miles south-west of Berwick-upon-Tweed on minor road off B6470 (from A698)
☎ (028982) 329
Open: Good Friday or beginning April-end September, daily 10am-6pm; beginning October-Maundy Thursday or end March, Tuesday-Sunday 10am-4pm; closed 24-26 December, 1 January.

Prudhoe Castle (EH)

Prudhoe, on minor road off A695
☎ (0661) 33459
Open: Good Friday or beginning April-end September, daily 10am-

6pm; beginning October-Maundy Thursday or end March, Tuesday-Sunday 10am-4pm; closed 24-26 December, 1 January.

St Paul's Monastery (EH)
Jarrow, on minor road north of A185
Open: any reasonable time.

Tynemouth Castle and Priory (EH)
In Tynemouth, near North Pier
☎ (091) 257 1090
Open: Good Friday or beginning April-end September, daily 10am-6pm; beginning October-Maundy Thursday or end March, Tuesday-Sunday 10am-4pm; closed 24-26 December, 1 January.
Gun Battery exhibition open pm Friday to Monday.

Warkworth Castle and Hermitage (EH)
$7^1/_2$ miles south of Alnwick on A1068
☎ (0665) 711423
Open: castle: Good Friday or beginning April-end September, daily 10am-6pm; beginning October-Maundy Thursday or end March, Tuesday-Sunday 10am-4pm; closed 24-26 December, 1 January. Hermitage: summer weekends only (access by boat $^1/_2$ mile upstream).

Accommodation

The Northumbria Tourist Board's annually updated Official Guide contains a comprehensive list of accommodation addresses, ranging from first class hotels to farmhouse bed and breakfast establishments and rented cottages.

Throughout the region Tourist Information Centres can help callers by provisionally finding accommodation. Most centres also have their own mini-guides covering their immediate district. Simple low-priced accommodation for families and groups, as well as individuals is available at any of the comprehensive range of youth hostels throughout Northumbria. Details of these are available in the *YHA Accommodation Guide* from MPC.

Boat Trips

Durham
Brown's Boat House, Elvet Bridge, Durham DH1 3AF
☎ (091) 386 9525
Rowing boat hire, launch trips on $3^1/_2$ miles of River Wear with fine views of the city.

Farne Islands
Sailings Easter-September. Charter trips and fishing cruises. All operators have offices on or near Seahouses quay.
☎ W. Sheil (0665) 720308; W. McKay (0665) 720155; H.J. Harvey (0665) 720388; J. Sheil (0665) 720825

Keilder Reservoir
Keilder Water Cruises, Tower Knowe, Yarrow Moor, Kielder
☎ (0660) 40436/20423
Ferry service and lake cruises. Operate from May-September. Telephone for further details.

Newcastle upon Tyne
River Tyne Cruises Limited, 2nd Floor Exchange Buildings, Quayside, Newcastle upon Tyne NE1 3BJ
☎ (091) 232 8683
Scheduled and charter trips along the river.

Sunderland
River Wear Ferry
☎ (091) 565 0960
River trips around the shipyards and to the Washington Wildfowl Centre.

Buildings and Gardens Open to the Public

As well as those properties listed below, many privately owned houses take part in the Northumbria Gardens Scheme and are open on specified dates. For further details, see annually published lists available from Tourist Information Centres.

Alnwick Castle
Close to Alnwick town centre
☎ (0665) 510777
Open: end April to early October, 1-5pm. (Closed Saturday end April-late June and September to early October).

Arcadia Nurseries
Brasscastle Lane, Nunthorpe, Middlesbrough TS8 9EB
☎ (0642) 310782
Open: 9am until dusk (8pm in summer).

Auckland Castle
Adjacent to Bishop Auckland town centre.
☎ (0388) 609766
State rooms and chapel open to the public.
Open: variable times, check locally.

Bamburgh Castle
Bamburgh, B1340 near Belford (A1)
☎ (06684) 208
Open: Easter-May bank holiday, daily 1-5pm; June-August, daily 12noon-6pm; September, daily 1-5pm; October, daily 1-4.30pm.

Belsay Hall (EH)
14 miles north-west of Newcastle upon Tyne, on A696
☎ (0661) 881636

Burnhall Gardens
St Joseph's Mission, Burnhall, Croxdale. A167, 5 miles south of Durham.
Open: Monday-Thursday 10am-4pm, Friday 10am-1pm; closed Saturday and Sunday.

Castle Keep
St Nicholas Street, Newcastle upon Tyne
☎ (091) 232 7938
Open: October-March 9.30am-4.30pm; April-September 9.30am-5.30pm. Closed every Monday except bank holiday Mondays, Christmas Day, Boxing Day and Good Friday.

Cathedral Treasury and College
Durham Cathedral
☎ (091) 384 4854
Open: Monday-Saturday 10am-4.30pm, Sunday 2-4pm all year round.

Chillingham Castle
Minor road off B6353 about 5 miles south-east of Wooler
☎ (06685) 390 or 359
Open: Easter-end September, 1.30-5pm daily except Tuesday.

Chillingham Wild Cattle Association
Parkland adjacent to Chillingham Castle
☎ (06685) 213
Open: Easter-October, daily except Tuesday and Sunday mornings, 10am-12noon, 2-5pm. No dogs allowed.

Cragside House (NT)
B6341, 2 miles north-east of Rothbury
☎ (0669) 20333
Open: house: beginning April-end October 1-5pm; closed Monday, open bank holiday Mondays. Grounds: beginning April-end October 10.30am-7pm (or dusk if earlier), daily; November-March 10.30am-4pm Saturday and Sunday.

Dial Cottage
Great Lime Road, Killingworth, Wallsend NE12 0BQ
Open: Easter-September, Tuesday-Friday 10am-5.30pm, Saturday 10am-4pm, Sunday 2-5pm. Closed Monday but open bank holidays.

Durham Castle
Palace Green, adjacent to the cathedral.
☎ (091) 374 3800
Open: July, August and September, daily 10.30am-4.30pm; October-June inclusive, Monday, Wednesday and Saturday 2-4.30pm.

Durham Cathedral
☎ (091) 386 2367
Open: October-April 7.30am-6pm; May-September 7.30am-8pm.

Eggleston Hall Gardens
B6278, Eggleston, 7 miles north-west of Barnard Castle
Open: as advertised locally.

Elsdon Tower
B6341, $3^1/_2$ miles east of Otterburn (A696)
☎ (0830) 20688
Open: grounds: end March-mid-September, 10am-6pm. House: open by appointment throughout the year.

Gateshead Central Nurseries
Whickham Highway, Lobley Hill NE11 9RQ
☎ (091) 460 0331
Open: any reasonable time.

Howick Gardens
Howick Hall; minor road between Longhoughton and Craster
☎ (066577) 285
Open: April-September, daily 2-7pm.

Hulne Park
Off B6346 near Alnwick
Open: Saturday and Sunday, daylight hours. A pass may be obtained for weekdays from the estate office.

Lindisfarne Castle (NT)
Open: Good Friday or beginning April-end September, daily except Friday 1-5.30pm; October, Saturday, Sunday, Wednesday, 1-5.30pm, last admission 5pm.

Meldon Park
Minor road linking B6343 and B6524, 11 miles south-west of Morpeth
☎ (067072) 661
Open: house: on advertised days in summer 2-5pm. Gardens: late May to end September, daily 2-5pm.

Monks Dormitory — Durham Cathedral
☎ (091) 386 2489
Open: as advertised. Telephone for details.

Neasham Gardens
Minor road linking A67 and A167, $4^1/_2$ miles south-east of Darlington
☎ (0325) 721405
Open: daily 10am until dusk.

Northumbria Nurseries
Castle Gardens, Ford TD15 2PZ;
B6353, 12 miles south-west of
Berwick-upon-Tweed.
☎ (089082) 379
Open: weekdays all year, 9am-
5pm, weekends March-October
and bank holidays, 1-5pm.

Ormesby Hall (NT)
Ormesby, near Middlesbrough
☎ (0642) 324188
Open: May-September, Wednesday, Thursday and Sunday
2-5.30pm; April and October,
Wednesday and Sunday 2-5.30pm,
last admission 5pm.

Penshaw Monument (NT)
Above A183 near Penshaw village.
Open: at all times.

Preston Tower
Ellingham, $^1/_2$ mile east of A1, 8
miles north of Alnwick
☎ (066589) 227
Open: daily during daylight hours.

Raby Castle
Staindrop, Darlington DL2 3AH
☎ (0833) 60202

Rokeby Park
Minor road linking A66 and
Barnard Castle (3 miles south-east
of latter).
☎ (0833) 27268
Open: Easter to end September,
Monday and Tuesday, 2-4.30pm.

Rookhope Nurseries
Rookhope, Upper Weardale
☎ (0388) 517272
Open: Easter-October 9am-5.30pm
daily; November-Easter 9.30am-
dusk.

St Aidan's College and Gardens
Windmill Hill, Durham
☎ (091) 374 3269

Open: daily during daylight hours.
Groups of ten and more by
appointment only.

St Mary's Lighthouse
Trinity Road, Whitley Bay
☎ (091) 252 0853
Open: Easter-end October as tides
permit; November-Easter open
school holidays and weekends.

Seaton Delaval Hall
Seaton Sluice, near Whitley Bay
☎ (091) 237 1493
Open: beginning May-end
September, Sunday, Wednesday
and bank holidays, 2-6pm.

**George Stephenson Birthplace
(NT)**
Wylam NE41 8PB
☎ (0661) 853457
Open: April-October, Wednesday,
Saturday and Sunday 1-5pm.

**University of Durham Botanical
Garden**
Hollingside Lane, Durham DH1
3TN
☎ (091) 374 2671
Open: all year, 10am-4pm.

**Wallington House and Walled
Garden (NT)**
Cambo, B6342, 20 miles north-west
of Newcastle upon Tyne.
☎ (067074) 283
Open: House: April-October daily
except Tuesday, 1-5.30pm (last
admission). Grounds: 10am-7pm
summer, 10am-4pm winter.

Washington Old Hall (NT)
The Avenue, District 4,
Washington NE38 7LE
☎ (091) 416 6879
Open: Good Friday and Easter
week, April-September, daily
except Friday 1-5.30pm (last

admission 5pm); October, Wednesday, Saturday and Sunday.

Hadrian's Wall

The following list covers those sites either fully or partially maintained by English Heritage; all are open to the public at specified times. The list also includes sites which lie in Cumbria.

Banks East Turret
On minor road east of Banks village, $3^1/_2$ miles north-east of Brampton. OS Map 86; ref NY575647.
Open: any reasonable time.

Benwell Roman Temple
Immediately south of A69 at Benwell in Broomridge Avenue. OS Map 88; ref NZ217646.
Open: any reasonable time.

Benwell Vallum Crossing
Immediately south of A69 at Benwell in Denhill Park Avenue. OS Map 88; ref NZ215646.
Open: any reasonable time.

Birdoswald Fort, Wall and Turret
(In the care of Cumbria County Council)
$2^3/_4$ miles west of Greenhead, on minor road off B6318. OS Map 86; ref NY615663.
Open: any reasonable time.

Black Carts Turret
2 miles west of Chollerford on B6318. OS Map 87; ref NY884712.
Open: any reasonable time.

Brunton Turret
$^1/_4$ mile south of Low Brunton on A6079. OS Map 87; ref NY922698.
Open: any reasonable time.

Carrawburgh: Temple of Mithras
$3^3/_4$ miles west of Chollerford on B6318. OS Map 87; ref NY869713.
Open: any reasonable time.

Cawfields Roman Wall and Milecastle
$1^1/_4$ miles north of Haltwhistle off B6318. OS Map 87; ref NY716667.
Open: any reasonable time.

Chesters Bridge Abutment
On east bank of North Tyne opposite Chesters Fort, on footpath from B6318 ($^1/_2$ mile). OS Map 87; ref NY914700.
Open: any reasonable time.

Chesters Fort and Museum
(Cilurnum)
$^1/_2$ mile west of Chollerford on B6318
☎ (0434) 681379
Open: Good Friday or beginning April-end September, daily 10am-6pm; beginning October-Maundy Thursday or end March, daily 10am-4pm; closed 24-26 December and 1 January.

Corbridge Roman Site
(Corstopitum)
$^1/_2$ mile north-west of Corbridge on minor road
☎ (0434) 632349
Open: Good Friday or beginning April-end September, daily 10am-6pm; Beginning October-Maundy Thursday or end March, Tuesday-Sunday 10am-4pm; closed 24-26 December and 1 January.

Denton Hall Turret
4 miles west of Newcastle city centre on A69. OS Map 88; ref NZ195656.
Open: any reasonable time.

Gilsland Vicarage Roman Wall
In former vicarage garden, Gilsland village, (B6318). OS Map 86; ref NY632662.
Open: any reasonable time.

Hare Hill
$^3/_4$ mile north-east of Lanercost, off minor road north-east of Brampton, (A69). OS Map 86; ref NY562646.
Open: any reasonable time.

Harrow's Scar Milecastle
$^1/_4$ mile east of Birdoswald Fort, $2^3/_4$ miles west of Greenhead, on minor road off B6318. OS Map 86; ref NY621664.
Open: any reasonable time.

Heddon-on-the-Wall
Immediately east of Heddon village, south of A69. OS Map 88; ref NZ136669. 280yd section of wall and medieval kiln.
Open: any reasonable time.

Housesteads Roman Fort
(Vercovicium)
Maintained jointly with the National Trust.
$2^3/_4$ miles north-east of Bardon Mill on B6318
☎ (0434) 344363
Joint National Trust — National Park Information Centre on main road.
Open: Good Friday or beginning April-end September, daily 10am-6pm; beginning October-Maundy Thursday or end March, daily 10am-4pm; closed 24-26 December and 1 January.

Lealhill Turret
On minor road 2 miles west of Birdoswald Fort. OS Map 86; ref NY585653.
Open: any reasonable time.

Pike Hill Signal Tower
On minor road east of Banks village. OS Map 86; ref NY577648.
Open: any reasonable time.

Piper Syke Turret
On minor road 2 miles west of Birdoswald Fort. OS Map 86; ref NY588654.
Open: any reasonable time.

Planetrees Roman Wall
1 mile south-east of Chollerford on B6318. OS Map 87; ref NY928696.
Open: any reasonable time.

Poltcross Burn Milecastle
Immediately south-west of Gilsland village, by old railway station. OS Map 86; ref NY634662.
Open: any reasonable time.

Sewingshields: Wall, Turrets and Milecastle
Minor road east of Housesteads Fort. OS Map 87; ref NY813702.
Open: any reasonable time.

Vindolanda Fort and Roman Milestone — Vindolanda Trust site.
$1^1/_4$ miles south-east of Once Brewed, on minor road off B6318.
Open: Good Friday or beginning April-end September, daily 10am-6pm; beginning October-Maundy Thursday or end March, Tuesday-Sunday 10am-4pm; closed 24-26 December and 1 January.

Wallsend Roman Fort
(Segedunum)
Wallsend town centre.
Open: any reasonable time.

Walltown Crags Wall and Turret
1 mile north-east of Greenhead off B6318. OS Map 87; ref NY674664.
Open: any reasonable time.

Willowford Bridge Abutment
West of minor road $^3/_4$ mile west of Gilsland. OS Map 86; ref NY629664.
Open: any reasonable time. (access via Willowford Farm; small charge).

Winshields: Wall and Milecastle
West of Steel Rigg car park, on minor road off B6318 (Once Brewed). OS Map 87; ref NY745676.
Open: any reasonable time.

Long Distance Footpaths

Castle Eden Walkway
Follows the abandoned railway line between Thorpe Thewles and Castle Eden. Suitable for cycles and also cross-country skiing in winter.

Derwent Valley Walkway
Footpaths linked to the old railway line from Consett to Whickham follow the wooded Derwent Valley.

Hadrian's Wall National Trail
Uses rights of way to follow Hadrian's Wall from coast to coast.

Pennine Way
Waymarked route from Edale in the Peak District to Kirk Yetholm in Scotland. Passes through a considerable portion of the higher parts of Northumbria.

Tyne Riverside Countrypark Footpaths
Historic railway trails near Prudhoe on the south bank and based on the Wylam Wallbottle Wagonway opposite.

Waskerley Way
High-level railway track from Rookhope to the outskirts of Consett.

Weardale Way
Using linking footpaths and byways, the route explores little known corners of upper Weardale. Route marked on the OS 1:25000 Outdoor Leisure Map No 2, Teesdale.

Museums, Art Galleries and Visitor Centres

Allenheads Heritage Centre
Allenheads NE47 9UQ
☎ (0434) 685395
Open: March-October 10am-5pm daily; October-March weekends only.

The Ankers House
The Parish Centre, Church Chare, Chester-le-Street DH3 3QB
☎ (091) 388 3295
Open: April-October 10am-4pm.

Arbeia Roman Fort and Museum
Baring Street, South Shields NE33 2BB
☎ (091) 456 1369 or 454 5199
Open: Tuesday-Friday 10am-5.30pm, Saturday 10am-4.30pm, Sunday (Easter-September only) 2-3pm. Closed Monday except bank holidays.

Bede Gallery
Springwell Park, Butchersbridge Road, Jarrow NE32 5QA
☎ (091) 489 1807
Art exhibitions.
Open: Tuesday-Friday 10am-5pm, Sunday 2-5pm. Closed Saturday, Monday and Christmas holidays.

Bede Monastery Museum

Jarrow Hall, Church Bank, Jarrow
NE32 3DY
☎ (091) 489 2106
Open: April-October, Tuesday-
Saturday 10am-5.30pm, Sunday
2.30-5.30pm; November-March,
Tuesday-Saturday 11am-4.30pm,
Sunday 2.30-5.30pm.

Berwick Barracks (EH)

Berwick-upon-Tweed TD15 1DF
☎ (0289) 304493
Open: Good Friday-end September, daily 10am-6pm; beginning
October-Maundy Thursday, daily
10am-4pm, but closed Mondays,
24-26 December and 1 January.

Berwick-upon-Tweed Museum and Art Gallery

The Barracks, Berwick-upon-
Tweed TD15 1DF
☎ (0289) 330933
Open: Easter-September Monday-
Saturday 10am-12.30pm, 1.30-6pm;
October-Easter Tuesday-Saturday
10am-12.30pm, 1.30-4pm.

Thomas Bewick Birthplace Museum

Cherryburn, Mickley, near
Stocksfield NE43 7DB (A695)
☎ (0661) 843276
Open: March-December, Tuesday-
Sunday, 10am-5pm.

Billingham Art Gallery

Billingham TS23 2LN
☎ (0642) 555443
Open: all year Monday-Saturday
9.30am-5pm. Closed Sundays.

Bill Quay Farm

Hainingwood Terrace, Bill Quay,
Gateshead
☎ (091) 438 5340
Open: all week 9am-5pm.

Binchester Roman Fort

Minor road 1 mile north of Bishop
Auckland
☎ (0388) 663089
Open: April-September 10.30am-
6pm. Closed Thursday and Friday.
For visits at other times, contact
Bowes Museum, ☎ (0833) 690606.

Bird Field Study Museum

Glanton, near Alnwick NE66 4AH
(A697, 10 miles south-west of
Wooler)
☎ (066578) 257
Open: daily July-August except
Wednesday. Guided tours 3pm
Saturday.

The Bowes Museum

Barnard Castle, DL12 8NP
☎ (0833) 690606
Open: all year except one week
prior to Christmas, and 1 January.
Monday-Saturday 10am-5.30pm,
Sunday 2-5pm. Closes 5pm March,
April, October and 4pm
November-February.

Bowlees Visitor Centre

B6277, 12 miles north-west of
Barnard Castle.

Buddle Arts Centre

258b Station Road, Wallsend NE28
8RH
☎ (091) 262 4276
Open: Tuesday-Friday 10am-9pm.
Saturday 10am-1pm, 2-5pm and
6-9pm.

D.G. Burleigh — bagpipe maker

Rothbury Road, Longframlington,
near Morpeth
☎ (066570) 635
Open: by appointment only.

Captain Cook Birthplace Museum

Stewart Park, Marton,
Middlesbrough TS7 8AS

☎ (0642) 311211
Open: winter 9am-4pm; summer
10am-6pm. Closed Mondays, open
Sundays. Last admission 45 min
before closing.

Castle Eden Dene Visitor Centre
Oakerside Dene Lodge, Stanhope
Chase, Peterlee SR8 1NJ
☎ (091) 586 0004
Open: 9am-5pm weekdays.
Various times at weekends, please
ring in advance.

Causey Arch
Beside A6076, $2^1/_2$ miles north of
Stanley
Open: any reasonable time.

**Chesterholme Museum
Vindolanda site**
Minor road 2 miles south of Once
Brewed (B6318)
☎ (0434) 344277
Open: daily February and November 10am-4pm; March and October
10am-5pm; April and September
10am-5.30pm; May and June 10am-
6pm; July and August 10am-
6.30pm.

Chesters Roman Fort (EH)
Chollerford (B6318)
☎ (0434) 681379
Open: Good Friday-end September, daily 10am-6pm; beginning
October-Maundy Thursday 10am-
4pm. Closed Mondays, 24-26
December and 1 January.

Corbridge Roman Fort (EH)
Adjacent to Corbridge town centre
☎ (04340) 632349
Open: Good Friday-end September
daily 10am-6pm; beginning
October-Maundy Thursday 10am-
4pm. Closed Mondays, 24-26
December and 1 January.

Grace Darling Museum
Radcliffe Road, Bamburgh NE69
7AE
Open: Easter weekend-early
October daily; April and September 11am-6pm; June, July and
August 11am-7pm.

Darlington Art Gallery
Crown Street, Darlington DL1 1ND
☎ (0325) 462034
Open: weekdays 10am-8pm,
Saturday 10am-5.30pm. Closed
bank holidays and preceeding
Saturdays.

Darlington Arts Centre
Vane Terrace, Darlington DL3 7AX
☎ (0325) 483271
Open: Monday-Saturday 9am-
11pm. Open bank holidays except
Christmas, New Year and Good
Friday.

Darlington Museum
Tubwell Row, Darlington DL1 1PD
☎ (0325) 463795
Open: Monday-Wednesday and
Friday 10am-1pm, 2-6pm. Closed
Christmas and New Year holidays,
also Good Friday and May Day.
Open other bank holidays.

**Darlington Railway Centre and
Museum**
North Road Station, Darlington
DL3 6ST
☎ (0325) 460532
Open: daily 9.30-5pm, last
admission 4.30pm. Closed
Christmas and New Year.

Dial Cottage
Great Lime Road, Killingworth,
near Wallsend NE12 0BQ
Open: Easter-September, Tuesday-
Friday 10am-5.30pm, Saturday
10am-4pm, Sunday 2-5pm. Open
bank holidays.

Dorman Museum

Linthorpe Road, Middlesbrough
TS5 6LA
☎ (0642) 813781
Open: Tuesday-Friday 10am-6pm,
Saturday 10am-5pm. Closed
Sunday and Monday.

Durham Heritage Centre

Saint Mary-le-Bow, Durham DH1
3ET
Open: Spring bank holiday to mid-
September, Saturday-Thursday
2-4.30pm.

Durham Light Infantry Museum and Arts Centre

Aykley Heads, Durham DH1 5TU
☎ (091) 384 2214
Open: Tuesday-Saturday 10am-
5pm, Sunday 2-5pm. Last
admission 4.30pm.

Durham University Oriental Museum

Elvet Hill (off South Road), DH1
3TH
☎ (091) 374 2911
Open: Monday-Saturday 9.30am-
1pm, 2-5pm, Sunday 2-5pm.
Closed weekends November-
February.

Earle Hill Museum

Wooler
☎ (0668) 81243
Open: May-October every Friday
afternoon and holiday weekends.

Forestry Commission Visitor Centre — Kielder Castle

Kielder, minor road 28 miles north-
west of Hexham
☎ (0660) 50209
Open: Easter-end September 10am-
5pm (bank holidays and August
10am-6pm).

Generations of Energy

Hartlepool Power Station
☎ (0429) 869201
Open: all year except Christmas
and bank holidays, Monday-Friday
9am-3.30pm. Evening visits and
power station tours by appointment.

Gray Art Gallery and Museum

Clarence Road, Hartlepool TS24
8BT
☎ (0492) 268916
Open: Monday-Saturday 10am-
5.30pm, Sunday 2-5pm. Closed
Christmas Day, Boxing Day and
New Year's Day

Greek Museum

Department of Classics, The
University, Newcastle upon Tyne
NE1 7RU
☎ (091) 222 6000
Open: 9.30am-4.30pm Monday-
Friday.

Green Dragon Museum

Theatre Yard, Stockton-on-Tees
TS18 1AT
☎ (0642) 674308
Open: all year, Monday-Saturday
9.30am-5pm.

Grindon Museum

Grindon Lane, Sunderland SR9
8HW
☎ (091) 528 4042
Open: all year 9.30am-6pm, except
Thursday, bank holidays and
preceeding Saturdays, Good
Friday, Christmas and New Year's
Day.

Timothy Hackworth Museum

Soho Cottage, Shildon DL4 1PQ
☎ (0388) 772036
Open: Friday, Saturday and
Sunday 10am-5pm, Easter, April-
June; September, Saturday and
Sunday, 10am-5pm.

Hall Hill Farm Visitor Centre
Lanchester DH7 0TA
☎ (0388) 730300
Open: Sunday before Easter, Good Friday, Easter Monday, Spring bank holiday to Summer bank holiday, 1-5pm.

Hamsterley Forest Visitor Centre
Minor roads 8 miles north of Barnard Castle.
☎ (038888) 312/646
Open: forest trails etc, all year. Visitor centre, March-September 10am-6pm weekdays, Saturday and Sunday 11am-5pm.

Hancock Museum
Barras Bridge, Newcastle upon Tyne
☎ (091) 222 7418
Open: 10am-5pm Monday-Saturday, 2-5pm Sunday.

Hartlepool Maritime Museum
Northgate, TS24 0LT
☎ (0429) 272814
Open: Monday-Saturday 10am-5pm. Closed Christmas Day, Boxing Day, New Year's Day and Good Friday.

Hatton Gallery
University of Newcastle upon Tyne NE1 7RU
☎ (0910) 222 6000
Open: weekdays 10am-5.30pm, Saturday (term time only) 10am-4.30pm. Closed Sunday.

House of Hardy Museum and Country Store
Willowburn (near Alnwick) NE66 2PG ☎ (0665) 602771
Open: Monday-Friday 9am-5pm, Saturday 10am-5pm.

Housesteads Roman Fort
B6318 Military Road, near Haydon Bridge NE47 6NN

☎ (0434) 344363
Open: Good Friday-end September, daily 10am-6pm; beginning October-Maundy Thursday 10am-4pm. Closed Mondays, 24-26 December and 1 January.

Jackson Dock
Victoria Terrace
☎ (0642) 266522 Ext 375
Open: Friday-Sunday only 2-4.30pm. Closed Christmas Day, Boxing Day, New Year's Day and Good Friday.

John George Joicey Museum
City Road, Newcastle upon Tyne NE1 2AS
☎ (091) 232 4562
Open: Tuesday-Friday 10am-5.30pm, Saturday 10am-4.30pm. Closed Sunday and Monday, except bank holidays which are 10am-4.30pm.

Killhope Wheel Lead Mining Centre
Upper Weardale (A689)
☎ (0388) 517272
Open: Easter-end October 10.30am-5pm.

Kirkleatham Old Hall Museum
Kirkleatham, near Redcar TS10 5NW
☎ (0642) 479500
Open: April-September 9am-5pm; October-March 10am-4pm. Closed Mondays (except bank holidays), Good Friday, 25 December-2 January.

Lady Waterford Hall
Ford Village, B6353, about 12 miles south-west of Berwick-upon-Tweed
☎ (089082) 224
Open: end March-end October, daily 10.30am-5.30pm; winter, by request.

Laing Art Gallery
Higham Place, Newcastle upon
Tyne NE1 8AG
☎ (091) 232 7734
Open: 10am-5.30pm Tuesday-
Friday, 10am-4.30pm Saturday,
2.30-5.30pm Sunday. Open bank
holiday Mondays.

Tom Leonard Mining Museum
Deepdale, Skinningrove, near
Saltburn
☎ (0287) 42877
Open: Easter-October 10am-4pm
daily, closed Saturday; November-
Easter 9.30am-3.30pm, closed
weekends.

Lindisfarne Priory Museum (EH)
Holy Island
☎ (0289) 89200
Open: Good Friday-end Septem-
ber, daily 10am-6pm; beginning
October-Maundy Thursday, daily
10am-4pm. Closed Mondays, 24-26
December, and 1 January.

The Little Museum of Gilesgate
The Vane-Tempest Hall, Gilesgate,
Durham DH1 1QG
Open: April-end September,
Saturday 10am-4pm, Sunday 2-
5pm.

**Middle March Centre for Border
History**
Manor Office, The Old Gaol,
Hallgate, Hexham NE46 3NH
☎ (04343) 604011 Ext 245
Open: Easter-early November,
Monday-Friday 10am-4.30pm;
July-August and first weekend in
September, also Saturday, 10am-
4.30pm, and Sunday 11am-4.30pm.

Middlesbrough Art Gallery
320 Linthorpe Road, Middlesbrough TS1 4AW
☎ (0642) 247445

Open: Tuesday-Saturday 10am-
6pm. Closed 1-2pm and between
exhibitions.

Military Vehicle Museum
Exhibition Park Pavilion, Newcastle upon Tyne
☎ (091) 281 7222
Open: daily 10am-2.30pm,
including a few hours on
Christmas and New Year's Day.

Monks Dormitory
Durham Cathedral, The College,
Durham DH1 3EH
☎ (091) 386 2489
Open: as advertised locally.

Monkwearmouth Station
North Bridge Street, Sunderland
SR5 1AP
☎ (091) 567 7075
Open: all year 10am-5pm, except
bank holidays, Christmas Day and
New Year's Day.

**Morpeth Chantry Bagpipe
Museum**
The Chantry, Bridge Street, NE61
1PJ
☎ (0690) 519466
Open: January-February 10am-
4pm, Monday-Saturday; March-
December 9.30am-5.30pm,
Monday-Saturday.

Morpeth Clock Tower
Oldgate, Morpeth
☎ (0670) 519664
Open: July-September, Saturdays
only 12noon-4pm.

Museum of Antiquities
The University, Newcastle upon
Tyne NE1 7RU
☎ (091) 222 6000
Open: 10am-5pm, daily Monday-
Saturday. Closed 24-26 December
and 1 January.

Museum of Archaeology
The Old Fulling Mill, The Banks,
Durham DH1 3EB
☎ (091) 374 3623
Open: April-October 11am-4pm;
November-March 1-3.30pm.

**Museum of Science
and Engineering**
Blandford House, Blandford Street,
Newcastle upon Tyne NE1 4JA
☎ (091) 232 6789
Open: Tuesday-Friday 10am-
5.30pm, Saturday 10am-4.30pm.
Closed Sunday and Monday.

Nenthead Mines and Museum
A689, 5 miles south-east of Alston
Open: any reasonable time.

**Nentsberry Mining and Farming
Museum**
A689, 3 miles south-east of Alston.
Open: daylight hours.

The New Elvet Gallery
7 New Elvet, Durham DH1 3AQ
☎ (091) 384 0081
Open: Monday-Saturday 10am-
5pm. Closed bank holidays.

Newburn Motor Museum
Townfield Gardens, Newburn,
near Newcastle upon Tyne
☎ (091) 264 2977

Newcastle Polytechnic Gallery
Library Building, Sandyford Road,
Newcastle upon Tyne NE1 8ST
☎ (091) 235 8424
Open: all year, Monday-Friday
10am-5pm, Saturday 10am-4pm.

Newham Grange Leisure Farm
Off B1365, south of Middlesbrough
☎ (0642) 245432
Open: Easter-end October 9.30am-
5pm; winter, Sundays only 9.30am-
dusk.

Norham Station Museum
Station House, Norham TD15 2LW
(B6470, 8 miles south-west of
Berwick-upon-Tweed)
☎ (028982) 217
Open: Easter weekend, all bank
holidays, June-mid-September,
Monday and Thursday 1.30-5pm.

North East Aircraft Museum
Washington Road, Sunderland SR5
3HZ
Open: all year 11am-6pm, except
bank holidays and Christmas.

**The North of England Open Air
Museum, Beamish**
Beamish, near Stanley DH9 0RG
☎ (0207) 231811
Open: beginning January-end
March, daily 10am-5pm, closed
Mondays; April-end October, daily
10am-6pm; November-March,
daily 10am-5pm. Check for
Christmas opening. Last admission
4pm.

**Once Brewed National Park
Visitor Centre**
Military Road, Once Brewed
☎ (0434) 344396
Open: March-October.

The Planetarium
South Tyneside College, St
George's Avenue, South Shields
NE34 6ET
☎ (091) 456 0403
Open: telephone for opening times.

Preston Park Museum
Yarm Road, Stockton-on-Tees TS18
3RH
☎ (0642) 781184
Open: all year.

Regimental Museum of the King's Own Scottish Borderers
The Barracks, Berwick-upon-Tweed TD15 1DG
☎ (0289) 307426/7
Open: daily 9.30am-4pm.

Roman Army Museum
Carvoran, Greenhead (B6318)
☎ (06972) 485
Open: every day March and October 10am-5pm; April and September 10am-5.30pm; May and June 10am-6pm; July and August 10am-6.30pm; November and February, Saturday and Sunday 10am-4pm. Closed December and January.

RNLI Zetland Lifeboat Museum
5 King Street, Redcar TS10 3PF
Open: daily including Sundays, 11am-4pm May-September.

Ryhope Engine Museum
Ryhope, near Sunderland SR2 0ND
☎ (091) 521 0235
Open: Saturday and Sunday, Easter-December 2-5pm. In steam Easter, Spring and August bank holidays.

St Peter's Church and Visitor Centre
St Peter's Way, Sunderland SR6 0DY
☎ (091) 567 3726
Open: any reasonable time.

Shipley Art Gallery
Prince Consort Road, Gateshead NE8 4JB
☎ (091) 477 1495
Open: Tuesday-Friday 10am-5.30pm, Saturday 10am-4.30pm, Sunday 2-5pm.

John Sinclair Railway Museum
Ford Forge, Heatherslaw (B6353, about 12 miles south-west of Berwick-upon-Tweed)
☎ (089082) 244
Open: June-September, daily 10am-5pm.

South Shields Museum
Ocean Road, South Shields NE33 2AU
☎ (091) 456 8740
Open: Tuesday-Friday 10am-5.30pm, Saturday 10am-4.30pm, Sunday 2-5pm. Closed Mondays except bank holidays.

Stephenson Railway Museum
Middle Engine Lane, North Shields
☎ (091) 262 2627
Open: all year; Tuesday-Friday 10am-5.30pm, Saturday 10am-4.30pm, Sunday 2-5pm. Closed Monday.

Sunderland Museum and Art Gallery
Borough Road, Sunderland SR1 1PP
☎ (091) 514 1235
Open: Tuesday-Friday 10am-5.30pm, Saturday 10am-4pm, Sunday 2-5pm. Closed Monday except bank holidays. Closed Christmas Day, New Year's Day and Good Friday.

Teesaurus Park
Riverside Park Road, Middlesbrough
Open: any reasonable time.

Trinity Maritime Centre
29 Broad Chare, Quayside, Newcastle upon Tyne NE1 3DQ
☎ (091) 261 4691
Open: 11am-4pm Tuesday-Saturday. Closed Sunday and Monday. By appointment Saturday.

Tynemouth Volunteer Life Brigade
Spanish Battery, Tynemouth NE30 4DD ☎ (091) 252 0933
Open: all year: Tuesday-Friday 10am-3pm, Sunday 10am-1pm. Closed Monday.

Wallsend Heritage Centre
Buddle Street, Wallsend NE28 6EH ☎ (091) 262 0012
Open: Tuesday-Friday 10am-5.30pm, Saturday 10am-4pm, Sunday 2-5pm.

Washington 'F' Pit Industrial Museum
Albany Way, District 2, Washington
☎ (091) 416 7640
Open: beginning April-end October, Tuesday-Friday 10am-5.30pm, Saturday 10am-4.30pm, Sunday 2-5pm. Closed Monday.

Weardale Folk Museum
High House Chapel, Ireshopeburn, near Stanhope.
☎ (0388) 53741
Open: May, June and September, Thursday, Saturday and Sunday; July-August, daily. Weekdays 1-5pm, Sundays 1-4pm. Also open Easter and bank holidays.

Wine and Spirit Museum and Chemist Shop Museum
Palace Green, Berwick-upon-Tweed TD15 1HR
☎ (0298) 305153
Open: Easter-end October. Closed Sundays.

Winlaton Cottage Forge
Church Street, NE21 6AR
☎ (091) 414 3223
Open: Monday, Tuesday, Thursday, Friday 10am-7.30pm. Wednesday 10am-5pm.

Woodhorn Church Museum
Woodhorn Village, near Ashington
☎ (0670) 817371
Open: Wednesday-Sunday and bank holidays, 10am-12.30pm and 1-4pm.

Woodhorn Colliery Museum
Woodhorn Village, near Ashington
☎ (0670) 856968
Open: Wednesday-Sunday and bank holidays, 10am-12.30pm and 1-4pm.

Wylam Railway Museum
Falcon Centre, Falcon Terrace, Wylam, near Newcastle upon Tyne NE41 8EE
☎ (0661) 852174
Open: Tuesday and Thursday 2-7.30pm, Saturday 9am-12noon. Open all year.

Nature Reserves and Country Parks

Allen Banks Woods (NT)
Near Bardon Mill
☎ (0434) 344218
Open: during daylight hours.

Bedlington Country Park
Church Lane, Bedlington NE22 5RT
☎ (0670) 829550
Open: any reasonable time.

Bolam Lake Country Park
Near Belsay
☎ (066181) 234
Open: at all times.

Breamish Valley Country Walks
Ingram, Powburn NE66 4LT
☎ (066578) 248 (information centre)
Open: at all times. Telephone information centre for details of guided walks.

Castle Eden Dene Nature Reserve
Peterlee
☎ (091) 586 0004 (Oakerside Dene visitor centre)
Open: reserve at all times. Visitor centre, 9am-8pm daily, by appointment only.

Coquet Island Nature Reserve (RSPB)
Amble-by-the-Sea
☎ (091) 232 4148

College Valley Estate
Near Wooler (private estate)
Open: by permit only, from John Sale and Partners, Wooler.

Collier Wood Picnic Area
A68, south of Tow Law, County Durham

Cragside Country Park (NT)
Near Rothbury
☎ (0669) 20333
Open: (park) daily, beginning April-end October 10.30am-7pm (or dusk if earlier); November-March, Saturday-Sunday 10.30am-4pm.

Cresswell Pond Nature Reserve and Visitor Centre
Cresswell, 4 miles south of Amble-by-the-Sea
Permits must be obtained from the visitor centre before visiting the pond.

Derwent Walk Country Park
Rowlands Gill
Two visitor centres, at Thornley Woodlands and Swalwell.

Druridge Bay Country Park
Hadston, 4 miles south of Amble-by-the-Sea
☎ (0670) 760968

Druridge Pools Nature Reserve
Druridge, 4 miles south of Amble-by-the-Sea
Day permits to visit may be obtained from Cresswell Pond visitor centre.

Farne Islands (NT)
Small group of islands 3 miles north of Seahouses.
Open: (breeding season), daily mid-May-mid-July, Staple Island 10.30am-1.30pm. Inner Farne 1.30-5pm. Out of season April-mid-May and mid-July-end September 10am-6pm.
☎ National Trust Centre: (0665) 70424; boatmen: W. Shiel (0665) 720308; W. McKay (0665) 720155; H.J. Harvey (0665) 720388; J. Shiel (0665) 720825
For birdwatching and botanical visits contact National Trust Warden, c/o The Shieling, 8 St Aidan's, Seahouses ☎ (0665) 72651.

Hardwick Hall Country Park
Sedgefield, County Durham
☎ (0740) 20745
Open: at all times.

Harthope Valley
Near Wooler
Open: any reasonable time.

Hauxley Nature Reserve and Visitor Centre
Low Hauxley, 4 miles south of Amble-by-the-Sea
☎ (0665) 711578
Open: 24 hours, but by day permits only — available 7 days a week 9am-5pm.

The Leas and Marsden Rock (NT)
South Shields
$2^1/_2$ miles of spectacular coastline from Trow Rocks to Lizard Point.

Newton Pool Nature Reserve (NT)
Beadnall Bay, $2^1/_2$ miles south-east of Seahouses.

Pow Hill Country Park
Derwent Reservoir, near Edmundbyers

Plessey Woods Country Park
Shields Road, Hartford, Bedlington
☎ (0670) 824793
Open: during daylight.

Queen Elizabeth 2 Country Park
Woodhorn, Ashington
☎ (0670) 856968
Open: all year.

Ryton Willows
Ryton, near Rowlands Gill.
Wooded riverside adjacent to attractive historic village.

Shibdon Pond Nature Reserve
Off Shibdon Road, Blaydon, Gateshead. Open: at all times.

Toytop Picnic Area
Alongside A68 between Darlington and West Auckland.

Tyne Riverside Country Park
Station Road Prudhoe
☎ (0661) 34135
Open: daylight hours.

Wansbeck Riverside Park
Ashington
☎ (0670) 812323
Open: any reasonable time.

Washingwell Wood
Between Gateshead and Sunniside.
Open: at all times.

The Wildfowl and Wetlands Centre
Washington District 15, Washington NE38 8LE
☎ (091) 416 5454
Open: daily 9.30-5pm, or dusk if earlier. Closed Christmas.

Other Places of Interest

Crowtree Leisure Centre
Crowtree Road, Sunderland SR1 3EL
☎ (091) 514 1511
Open: varied according to facilities required.

Escomb Church
Escomb village, near Bishop Auckland, County Durham.
Open: daylight hours. (Key from 22 Saxon Green behind the church).

Gateshead International Stadium
Neilson Road, Gateshead
☎ (091) 478 1687

Gateshead Leisure Centre
Alexandra Road, Gateshead NE8 4JA
☎ (091) 477 3939
Open: all week 8am-10pm.

Gateshead Metrocentre
Off A69
Metroland — Metrocentre
Indoor theme park. Rides, waterfalls and other attractions.
☎ (091) 493 2048
Metrocentre Cinema
Ten screen cinema
☎ (091) 493 2023
GX Superbowl Metrocentre
28 lane bowling alley
☎ (091) 493 2046

Gibside Chapel (NT)
Burnopfield, off B6314, south of Rowlands Gill
☎ (0207) 542255
Open: beginning April-end October, Tuesday-Sunday 11am-5pm.

Heatherslaw Corn Mill
B6354, Ford, 10 miles south-west of
Berwick-upon-Tweed
☎ (089082) 338 summer only.
Open: daily, Easter-end October
10am-6pm.

Lady's Well (NT)
Holystone, minor road 7 miles west
of Rothbury.
Open: at all times.

Leap Mill Farm
Burnopfield NE16 6BJ
☎ (0207) 71375
Open: end March-end October,
Sundays 2-6pm.

**Lordenshaws — Cup and Ring
marks**
Moorland near Rothbury,
(NZ052991)

Stewart Park Children's Zoo
Ladgate Lane, Middlesbrough

Thirlwall Castle
Greenhead, near Haltwhistle
On private land, but permission to
view is usually granted.

Tockett's Water Mill
Skelton Road, near Guisborough
☎ (0287) 39285
Open: end May-end September,
Sundays.

Tyne Theatre and Opera House
Westgate Road, Newcastle upon
Tyne NE1 4AG
☎ (091) 232 1551

Whorlton Lido
Minor road 4 miles south-east of
Barnard Castle
☎ (0833) 27397
Open: Easter-September, daily
(weekends only in September)
10am-6pm or 7pm during the high
season.

Winter's Gibbet
South-east of Elsdon

Yeavering Bell
B6351, 4 miles north-west of
Wooler

Steam Railways

Beamish Open-Air Museum
Beamish, near Stanley
☎ (0207) 231811
Open: beginning January-end
March, daily 10am-5pm, closed
Mondays; April-October, daily
10am-6pm; November-March,
daily 10am-5pm, closed Mondays.

Bowes Railway
Springwell Village, Gateshead NE9
7QJ
Open: bank holiday weekends,
Sunday-Monday. Alternate
Sundays in June, July and August,
and beginning of September,
10am-4.30pm.

Heatherslaw Light Railway
Ford Forge. B6354, 10 miles south-
west of Berwick-upon-Tweed
☎ (089082) 350
Open: April-October, daily
10am-6pm.

**South Tynedale Railway
Preservation Society**
Alston, on A686
☎ (0498) 81696
Trains at weekends Easter-
September; daily during summer
months. Shop, café, tourist
information, parking Alston
Station.

Tanfield Railway
Marley Hill, Sunniside, Gateshead
NE16 5ET
Open: Easter-December, Monday-

Friday 10am-4pm, Saturday-Sunday 10am-5pm.

Whorlton Lido
Minor road 4 miles south-east of Barnard Castle
☎ (0833) 27397
Open: Easter-September (weekends only in September), daily. Low season 10am-6pm; high season 10am-7pm.

Tourist Information Centres

Those centres which are marked with an asterisk * are closed in winter.

Northumbria Tourist Board
Aykley Heads, Durham DH1 5UX
☎ (091) 384 6905

Northumberland

Alnwick
The Shambles, NE66 1TN
☎ (0665) 510665

Amble
Council Sub Offices, Dilston Terrace, NE65 0DT
☎ (0665) 712313 *

Belford
2 & 3 Market Place, NE70 7ND
☎ (06683) 888

Bellingham
Main Street, Bellingham, Hexham NE48 2BQ
☎ (0434) 220616 *

Berwick-upon-Tweed
Castlegate Car Park, TD15 1JS
☎ (0298) 330733

Corbridge
The Vicar's Peel, NE45 5AW
☎ (0434) 623815 *

Haltwhistle
Tynedale District Sub-Office, Sycamore Street, NE49 0AG
☎ (0434) 320351 *

Hexham
Manor Office, Hallgate, NE46 1XD
☎ (0434) 605225

Kielder
Tower Knowe, Falstone, Hexham NE48 1BX
☎ (0660) 40398

Morpeth
The Chantry, Bridge Street, NE61 1PJ
☎ (0670) 511323

Once Brewed
National Park Information Centre, Military Road, Bardon Mill, Hexham NE47 7AN
☎ (0434) 344396 *

Otterburn
Percy Arms Hotel, Jedburgh Road, NE19 1NR
☎ (0830) 20261 *

Rothbury
National Park Information Centre, Church Street, NE65 7LP
☎ (0669) 20887 *

Seahouses
Car Park, Seafield Road, NE68 7SR
☎ (0665) 720884 *

Wooler
High Street car park, NE71 8LD
☎ (0668) 81602 *

Tyne and Wear

Gateshead
Central Library, Prince Consort Road, NE8 4LN
☎ (091) 477 3478

Gateshead Metro Centre
Portcullis, 74 Russell Way NE11 9YG ☎ (091) 460 6345

Jarrow
Jarrow Hall, Church Bank, NE32 3DY
☎ (091) 489 2106

Newcastle upon Tyne
City Information Service, Central Library, Princess Square, NE99 1DX
☎ (091) 261 0691

Newcastle Airport
Woolsington, NE13 8BU
☎ (091) 271 1929

North Shields
Tyne Commission Quay, North Shields Ferry Terminal, NE29 6EN
☎ (091) 257 9800

South Shields
South Shields Museum, Ocean Road, NE33 2HZ
☎ (091) 6612

South Foreshore, NE33 2LB
☎ (091) 455 7411 *

Sunderland
Crowtree Leisure Centre, Crowtree Road, SR1 3EL
☎ (091) 5650960 & 5650990

Whitley Bay
Park Road, NE26 1EJ
☎ (091) 252 4494

County Durham

Barnard Castle
43 Galgate, DL12 8EL
☎ (0833) 690909

Darlington
Darlington District Library, Crown Street, DL1 1ND
☎ (0325) 469858

Durham City
Market Place, DH1 3NI
☎ (091) 384 3720

Peterlee
20 The Upper Chare, SR8 5TE
☎ (091) 586 4450

Shotley Bridge
1 Church Bank, Shotley Bridge, Consett DH8 0HF
☎ (0207) 591043

Cleveland

Guisborough
Fountain Street, TS14 6QF
☎ (0287) 33801

Hartlepool
Leisure Services Department, Civic Centre, Victoria Road, TS24 8AY
☎ (0429) 266522

Middlesbrough
51 Corporation Road, TS1 1LT
☎ (0642) 243425 & 245432 (ext 3580)

Redcar
Regent Cinema Building, Newcomen Terrace, TS10 1AU
☎ (0642) 471921

Saltburn
4 Station Buildings, Station Square, TS12 1AQ
☎ (0287) 22422

Stockton
Theatre Yard, off High Street, TS18 1AT
☎ (0642) 615080

OTHER INFORMATION CENTRES
The following National Park and National Trust Information Centres can offer specialist advice for their locality. Many are the venue for organised walks and other events — see the National Park annual news sheet and local notices. Some are only open during the summer.

National Trust
Craster
Car park, Craster, Alnwick
☎ (067 074) 691

Holy Island
Lindisfarne Information Centre,
Elm House, Mary Gate, Holy
Island
☎ (0289) 89253

Housesteads
Housesteads car park, Military
Road, Bardon Mill, Hexham
☎ (04984) 525

Rothbury
Cragside
☎ (0669) 20333

Cowhaugh Car Park
☎ (0669) 20333

Wallington
East Coach House, Wallington
Courtyard, Canbo
☎ (067 074) 673

National Park
Cawfields
Hadrian's Wall

Harbottle
near Morpeth

Ingram
Ingram, Powburn, near Alnwick
☎ (0665) 78248

Once Brewed
Once Brewed, Military Road, near
Bardon Mill
☎ (04984) 396

Rothbury
Church House, Church Street
☎ (0669) 20887

Useful Addresses

English Heritage
Northern Region
The Castle
Carlisle
Cumbria CA3 8UR
☎ (0228) 31777

Forestry Commission
Kielder Forest District
Eals Burn
Bellingham, Hexham
Northumberland NE48 2AJ
☎ (0660) 20242

Forestry Commission
Rothbury District Forest
1 Walby Hill
Rothbury, Morpeth
Northumberland NE65 7NT
☎ (0669) 20569

National Trust
Scots' Gap
Morpeth
Northumberland NE61 4EG
☎ (067074) 691

Northumberland National Park
Eastburn
South Park, Hexham
Northumberland NE46 1BS
☎ (0434) 605555

INDEX

A Note to the Reader

We hope you have found this book informative, helpful and enjoyable. It is always our aim to make our publications as accurate and up to date as possible. With this in mind, we would appreciate any comments that you might have. If you come across any information to update this book or discover something new about the area we have covered, please let us know so that your notes may be incorporated in future editions.

As it is MPC's principal aim to keep our publications lively and responsive to change, any information that readers provide will be a valuable asset to us in maintaining the highest possible standards for our books.

Please write to:
Senior Editor
Moorland Publishing Co Ltd
Free Post
Ashbourne
Derbyshire
DE6 9BR